D1045257

CHICAGO PUBLIC LIBRARY

The New
New Left

STEVEN MALANGA

The New
New Left

How American Politics
Works Today

. . . .

Ivan R. Dee
Chicago 2005

www.ivanrdee.com

Most of the contents of this book appeared originally in *City Journal*, published by The Manhattan Institute.

Library of Congress Cataloging-in-Publication Data:
Malanga, Steven
    The new new left : how American politics works today / Steven Malanga.
        p. cm.
    Most of the contents of this book originally appeared in City journal.
    Includes index.
    ISBN 1-56663-644-2 (hc : alk. paper)
    1. United States—Economic policy. 2. United States—Social policy.
3. Right and left (Political science) I. City journal (New York, N.Y.) II. Title.
    HC106.83.M34 2005
    330.973—dc22

                                                              2004027461

To my mother and father,

who set me on the right path,

and to Wendi,

who keeps me there

Contents

Introduction: Tax Eaters versus Taxpayers   9

1   Round One: The "Living Wage"   21

2   Union U.   38

3   Why Wal-Mart Is the Enemy   51

4   The Prophets of Victimology   70

5   The Curse of the Creative Class   90

6   Who Really Runs New York?   107

7   A Council of Dunces   118

8   The Antidote: A Free Market at Work   133

Index   149

The New
New Left

Introduction:
Tax Eaters
versus Taxpayers

Politics in America today is not only a contest between left and right. A new political dynamic has slowly been emerging over the past forty years, a face-off between those who benefit from an expanding government and those who must pay for it—the tax eaters versus the taxpayers. The vast expansion of the public sector is finally reaching a tipping point, giving tax eaters the upper hand, especially in America's cities. There, coalitions of public employees, staffers at publicly funded social-services programs, and the recipients of government aid have emerged as effective new political forces. In New York City, for example, they have helped roll back some of the reforms of the Giuliani years. In California cities and towns they are thwarting the expansion of private businesses, Wal-Mart above all. In nearly a hundred municipalities they have imposed higher costs on tens of thousands of businesses by persuading city councils to pass "living-wage" laws.

This increasingly powerful public-sector movement results from the joining together of two originally distinct forces. First are the government-employee unions, born in the 1950s and nowadays the eight-hundred-pound gorillas of policy debates in many statehouses and city councils. Today public unions don't merely use their power to win contract concessions for their members. They help elect sympathetic legislators and defeat proponents of smaller government; they lobby for higher taxes, especially on the rich and on businesses; and they oppose legislative efforts, such as privatization initiatives, aimed at making government smaller and more efficient.

For years, government employees had no right to organize, on the grounds that there was no competition in the delivery of government services and that therefore public unions could hold cities and states hostage by going on strike and denying essential services to the public. Even some private-sector union leaders questioned the wisdom of letting public-sector workers organize and giving them the right to strike. But that began to change in the mid-1950s, when the American Federation of State, County and Municipal Employees (AFSCME) began lobbying for the right of local workers to organize and bargain collectively. The organization scored its first major victory in 1958 when it persuaded New York City mayor Robert Wagner, looking to cultivate and strengthen his union support, to give municipal workers collective bargaining rights. Over the next several years, other states and cities, especially those with strong union movements, passed laws allowing public employees to unionize. Buoyed by these victories, AFSCME's membership rose from 100,000 in 1955 to 250,000 by 1965 and to more than 1 million by 1985.

Other government-employee organizations followed AFSCME's lead. In 1960 the American Federation of Teachers mapped out a controversial strategy to win collective bargaining rights for teachers around the country, using Mayor Wagner and labor-friendly New York City as a test case. Although New York City's first teachers' walkout, in November 1960, had little public support, the union movement gained adherents among teachers nationwide, so that over the next five years there were thirty-six strikes against municipal school systems. In 1966 alone, another three dozen strikes occurred, as teacher militancy rose in places such as Newark, Baltimore, and Youngstown, Ohio. Meanwhile, from 1960 through 1966 membership in the AFT more than doubled to 136,000.

In retrospect, most of the warnings voiced about public-employee unions in those tumultuous years have proven accurate. Political leaders and labor experts predicted that government-employee unions would use their power over public services to win contracts with work rules far more generous and undemanding than in the private sector; and that without the restraints on salaries and benefits that the free marketplace imposes on private firms, unions would win increasingly meaty compensation packages that would be impossible to restrain or to roll back once enacted.

But what critics did not anticipate was how far public-employee unions would move beyond collective bargaining to inject themselves into the electoral and legislative processes. Today the endorsement of a public-sector union is crucial to the election of many local candidates, and public unions now often spend far more on lobbying and political advertising on local issues than any business group does. Nor could the critics have envisioned a time when a shrinking private-sector union movement would forge alliances with the public sector, and when the lines between the two would increasingly blur, as formerly private-sector unions, such as the Service Employees International Union, would slowly come to represent growing numbers of health-care and other workers, whose jobs depend on public money.

Reinforcing the public-employee unions in the powerful new coalition of tax eaters are the social-services groups created by the War on Poverty. Nominally private, they are sustained by and organized around public funding. Before the War on Poverty, most social-services agencies were privately organized and funded and had little stake in government spending policies. Groups like Catholic Charities, for example, received less than 10 percent of their support from government sources. But all that changed beginning in 1965, when federal spending on social services soared, increasing from $800 million to $2.2 billion between 1965 and 1970, and then soaring to $13 billion by 1980. This flood of money transformed many formerly private welfare organizations into government contractors, and their employees into quasi-public workers. It also spurred the creation of vast new networks of such organizations, as social-services entrepreneurs conjured into being a constellation of housing groups, subsidized day-care centers, employment-training programs, health clinics, and much more—all designed to tap into the new War on Poverty money.

This social-services funding vastly expanded the publicly supported workforce almost overnight. Before the 1970s the government didn't even count private social services as a sector, because it was so small. But in 1972 a Bureau of Labor Statistics employment census of the industry found 550,000 people working in the sector. By 1980 that number had more than doubled to 1.1 million. The sector's upward arc has continued unabated since then, with especially fast growth during the 1990s. Today the field teems with some 3.3 million workers, most of them supported by government-funded programs. Whereas in the early 1970s private social services accounted for less than 1 percent of the American workforce, today it accounts for 3 percent of jobs.

Because the clientele for social services is concentrated in the big cities, much of the growth in social-services employment has taken place there too. In New York, for example, social-services jobs increased from 52,000 to 183,000 between 1975 and 2000, so that by the end of the millennium more New Yorkers were employed in social services than on Wall Street. In Philadelphia, from 1988 (the first year that numbers are available) to 2000, social-services jobs more than doubled to nearly 30,000. In Boston during that same period, these jobs increased by 67 percent to nearly 55,000, while in Chicago they grew by nearly 140 percent to 83,000. In all these cases, social-services employment grew much faster than the cities' economies as a whole. And cities poured their own funds into such programs to augment (much greater) federal spending, especially in the early 1980s, when the Reagan administration restrained the growth of federal social-services programs. New York City, for instance, increased its spending on programs for the homeless from $8 million in 1978, two years before Reagan beat Jimmy Carter, to $100 million annually by 1985. In the early 1980s, New York State increased its spending on alcohol and drug addiction programs alone by two-thirds to nearly $500 million.

Almost from the War on Poverty's inception, these social-services employees and their clients began to show themselves a powerful political force, as when New York welfare workers in the early 1970s mobilized recipients to storm government offices demanding higher benefits. Some social-services agencies organized their employees and clients into grassroots political operations, parlaying their huge empires built on government and foundation money into political power. Ramon Velez, for example—whose Bronx network of government-funded health centers, alcoholism clinics, and other programs garnered over $300 million in government money over twenty-five years—engineered the election of several city council and state assembly members in the Bronx, and Velez himself served on New York's city council.

At the same time the War on Poverty was getting under way and federal spending on social services was beginning to soar, the Johnson administration created the two gigantic health-care programs, Medicaid and Medicare, providing care to the poor and to the elderly, respectively. In the process, Washington vastly changed the economics of U.S. medical care, turning it increasingly into a government-funded industry. From the very start, Medicaid and Medicare, initiated within a year of each other, cost far more than anyone had expected, because they encouraged overuse of the health-care system, prompted overbilling by doctors and hospitals, and led to widespread fraud. In fewer than five years the federal budget for Medicaid rose to $6 billion from just $1.2 billion in its first year, 1966, while expenditures by the states, which shared the program's cost with the federal government, also ballooned. With so much new money pouring into it, the size of the country's health-care industry exploded. In the entire decade before the federal programs began, U.S. health-care employment had increased by about 800,000 jobs, but in the first ten years of Medicaid and Medicare, the growth rate more than doubled, and the industry added more than 2 million new jobs, including more than 1 million in hospitals.

The new federal programs made many hospitals dependents of the state, especially in cities with the largest Medicaid populations. Within a few years, urban hospitals that had previously received very little federal money were living principally on Medicaid and Medicare payments. And once government had become a prime payer in the health-care system, hospitals that had low occupancy rates or duplicated services provided by other local institutions could survive on government payments rather than being forced to close. Such institutions could gold-plate their treatments of patients in order to increase revenues, so that hospitalizations and length of hospital stays increased. As a result, by 1980—to take only one example—experts estimated that New York City had five thousand more occupied hospital beds than it really needed. Also as a result, at least in part, health-care jobs grew from 3.9 percent of the U.S. private workforce in 1965 to nearly 10 percent today.

Shrinking the bloated system and stemming such abuses became politically impossible. Above all, what would become of all those who were employed in hospitals that should be closed?

The gradual government takeover of health care—a process continuing to this day—has transformed the industry's institutions, executives, and workers into unremitting lobbyists for ever greater public monies and expanding programs, and tireless foes of efforts to restrain costs. Hospitals and health-care unions were the chief opponents of the Gingrich Congress's efforts to balance the federal budget in the mid-1990s in part by cutting the growth of Medicaid and Medicare, and they derailed some of the steepest proposed cuts. At the state and local levels, especially in cities where the industry heavily depends on Medicaid and Medicare, hospitals and hospital workers have become two of the most influential power blocs. In New York State, for instance, a coalition of hospitals and unions spent $13 million in 1999, a record for Albany, lobbying to turn back cuts in the state's huge Medicaid system. Dennis Rivera, the head of Local 1199, a New York City–based union of health-care workers, has become the most powerful union leader in the state, far more influential than the head of the state AFL-CIO.

The electoral activism of this New New Left coalition of tax eaters—public-employee unions, hospitals and health-care-worker unions, and social-services agencies—has reshaped the politics of many cities. As the country's national political scene has edged rightward, thwarting their ambitions in Washington, these groups have turned their attention to urban America, where they still have the power to influence public policy. Looking over the electoral map of the United States, one sees that the nation's cities are the most blue, even in states that are otherwise politically red.

Increasingly in cities around the country, the road to electoral success passes through the public-employee/health/social-services sector. In New York City, for instance, more than two-thirds of city council members are former government employees or ex-workers in health care or social services. The first Latino speaker of the California State

Assembly, Antonio Villaraigosa—who narrowly lost the 2001 election for mayor of Los Angeles and served as a national co-chair of John Kerry's presidential campaign—is a former organizer for the Los Angeles teachers' union. Jane Campbell, the current mayor of Cleveland, snapped up a $3,000 grant back in 1974 to start WomenSpace, a women's advocacy group, and used her role as executive director of the organization to launch a twenty-year career in elective office in Ohio. Kansas City mayor Kay Barnes entered public life working as a paid staffer in the 1960s for the Cross-Lines Cooperative, a local social-services network, and she later helped found and run the Women's Resource Service, an advocacy center on the campus of the University of Missouri–Kansas City.

One reason why these politicians have succeeded electorally is that those who work in the tax-eater sector clearly have different voting priorities from private-sector workers or business owners. An exit poll of the 2001 New York City mayoral election, conducted by the Manhattan Institute's *City Journal*, found that private-sector workers heavily backed Michael Bloomberg, the businessman candidate who had been endorsed by Rudy Giuliani and had run on a pledge of no new taxes (which he abandoned after his first year in office), while those who worked in the public/health/social-services sectors favored his Democratic opponent, who ran on a promise of raising taxes to fund further services. In the race, Bloomberg won among private-sector voters by 17 percentage points while the Democrat won by 15 points among those who work in the public/nonprofit sectors.

And, of course, public-sector workers, who realize they are going to the polls to elect their bosses, make sure to remember to vote. Although they make up about one-third of New York City's workforce, public/nonprofit-sector voters made up 37 percent of the electorate in the New York City 2001 mayoral race. Minority workers who earn their living in the public sector were dramatically more likely than their private-sector counterparts to vote.

With so much of their economic future at stake in elections, the tax eaters have emerged as the new infantry of political campaigns, replacing the ward captains and district leaders of old-time political clubs. Today it's the members of the New New Left, through their unions and community-based organizations, who are most likely to run political phone banks, distribute campaign literature, and run get-out-the-vote efforts for their favored candidates. Indeed, when a member of Local 1199 ran for Gotham's city council in 2003, a local Democratic politician noted admiringly that the candidate, through her union colleagues, could field "a million foot soldiers." And, like the old Tammany Hall and other urban political machines, these efforts have sparked controversy. Members of the New New Left advocacy group ACORN (Association for Community Reform Now), which ran aggressive voter-registration drives in many cities during the 2004 elections, were accused of submitting fake or forged registrations in places such as Duluth, Cincinnati, and St. Petersburg, Florida.

Perhaps it's not surprising that the urban left has evolved into so narrow a movement, promoting no more than its own self-interest. Although it started out as a romantic but wrongheaded idea, the War on Poverty was the child of idealists who really believed that a benevolent, paternalistic government could offer solutions that America's private economy couldn't provide for the poor. But the most cherished ideals and programs of the movement have turned out to be demonstrably wrong, and many Americans now reject them. Unlimited welfare proved an economic and social disaster, producing an underclass of perpetual recipients who after years on the dole felt incapable of functioning as productive citizens. Liberalization of the criminal laws and judicial leniency, part of a War on Poverty mind-set that saw criminals as victims of society, only led to soaring crime rates, which drove law-abiding citizens out of cities and condemned those who could not leave to a life of fear. Government-funded alcohol and drug rehabilitation programs that placed little emphasis on personal responsibility and individual redemption had zero effect on the rise of addiction.

By the mid-1990s, Americans were eager for reform, and they got it. Changes in welfare law that imposed time limits on assistance and required recipients to work have turned out to be a great success, reducing public assistance rolls and getting millions of people back to work, without raising the poverty rate. Tough, activist policing innovations have vastly reduced crime, freeing millions of Americans, especially those in inner cities, from fear.

In the face of such results, the new urban left has emerged as an increasingly cynical coalition, ever more focused on goals that benefit its members and their allies, even though it retains the jargon of "social justice." The living-wage movement has largely been promoted by unions more interested in laws that bolster union membership and derail privatization or other attempts to make government more efficient than in legislation that genuinely helps the poor. Many of the living-wage laws enacted around the country exempt unionized companies from adhering to wage guidelines. Similarly, university-based labor programs, most of them at publicly funded institutions, have all but abandoned the principles of objective research and disinterested instruction and have transformed themselves into co-conspirators of organized labor, producing bogus "research studies" and engaging in partisan advocacy to advance the cause. Legislative bodies commandeered by these advocates have cynically enacted laws that have been a boon to their allies but have harmed the cities themselves, as, for example, the New York city council's passage of a living-wage law that raised the wages of home health-care workers but cost the city and state millions of dollars—in the midst of the city's worst budget crisis ever. In municipalities throughout California, to take another example, the coalition has successfully advocated for laws that restrict consumers' choices by making it difficult for Wal-Mart and other nonunion retailers to open in places where unionized stores currently predominate.

Regardless of how transparent its aims now seem, this new coalition will remain formidable because the tax-eater sector is now so large in many cities and states that it can easily thwart reforms aimed at undermining its programs. With much of its legislative agenda merely concerned with expanding programs and enacting laws that add to its own numbers, the New New Left may be in the ascendancy for a long time to come.

ONE

. . . .

Round One: The "Living Wage"

Over the past decade, a savvy left-wing political movement, supported by radical economic groups, liberal foundations, urban activists, and public-employee unions, has lobbied for a government-guaranteed "living wage" for low-income workers, considerably higher than the current minimum wage. The movement has scored enormous success: about one hundred cities nationwide, from New York to San Francisco, now have living-wage legislation in place. Many of the earliest laws were narrowly focused on workers at companies with government contracts. But as the movement has grown, it has successfully imposed its mandate on a wider array of businesses; one city has even passed a citywide living wage.

This is bad news for cities. The living wage poses a big threat to their economic health because the costs and restrictions it imposes on the private sector will destroy

jobs—especially low-wage jobs—and send businesses fleeing to other locales. Worse still, the living-wage movement's
agenda doesn't end with forcing private employers to increase wages. It includes opposing privatization schemes,
strong-arming companies into unionizing, and other economic policies equally harmful to urban health.

The living-wage movement got its start in mid-1990s
Baltimore, whose radical urban politics and anti-business
ethos provided fertile ground. In 1993 a coalition of Baltimore's left-leaning church leaders, unionists, and community activists began to push for a "social compact" that
included a hike in the minimum wage to $6.10—43 percent
above the federal minimum wage at the time—for service
workers in hotels and other businesses in the city's redevel-
oped Inner Harbor, a prime tourist area.

Baltimore's then-mayor Kurt Schmoke initially balked
at the potential damage that such a wage increase would
inflict on the city's already shrinking economy and budget.
But he eventually signed a compromise bill that guaranteed the new $6.10 minimum for workers at any compa-
nies contracting with the city, on the principle that, unlike
the Inner Harbor firms, these employers benefited directly
from public funds and thus had an obligation to pay a
higher minimum as a way of helping the city carry out its
self-proclaimed mission of improving the lot of the urban
poor.

Supporters hailed the increase as a costless victory for
low-income workers. The labor-backed Preamble Center for
Public Policy rushed out a study purporting to show that
the legislation benefited Baltimore workers but did no
harm to the local economy or to the city budget because city
contractors effortlessly absorbed the cost of the wage hike.

The study's claims didn't withstand scrutiny—contracting costs did rise—but that was almost beside the point. Far from turning into a workers' paradise, Baltimore saw its economy crash and burn during the mid-1990s, with 58,000 jobs disappearing, even as the rest of Maryland added 120,000 jobs and other cities across the country prospered. The living-wage bill was just one expression of a fiercely anti-business climate that helped precipitate Baltimore's economic collapse.

Sensible observers would call Baltimore in the nineties an urban disaster, but to the nascent living-wage movement the city became the poster child for future activism. Looking to the "success" of the living-wage campaign in Baltimore, a host of left-wing groups, including Ralph Nader's Citizens Action and ACORN, joined forces in 1995 in a national "Campaign for an America That Works," which made the living wage central to its demands. The campaign was so radical that it had no impact at the national level. But on the local level, where the political environment is usually far to the left of Washington, it popularized the living-wage idea, which began to catch on in city after city.

As it spread beyond Baltimore, the living-wage movement at first purposely kept its aims narrow. Early legislative victories applied to just a few workers. In 1996, for example, Milwaukee County passed a law increasing the minimum wage only for city-contracted janitors and security guards to $6.25 an hour. New York City's law, passed over Mayor Giuliani's veto, applied only to government-contracted security personnel, cleaning workers, and temporary employees.

Soon, though, living-wage supporters began to win ever broader laws, covering ever more workers and businesses.

Detroit's 1998 living wage applied to any business or non-profit with a city contract or to any firm that had received $50,000 or more in economic development assistance—ranging from the Salvation Army to small manufacturers located in the city's economic development zones. San Francisco's law went beyond city contractors to cover workers at the city airport, on the grounds that businesses there leased land from the city; airlines, newsstands, fast-food restaurants—none was exempt. In early 2002, New Orleans, ACORN's national home, enacted the first citywide living wage in the nation—something that the movement would like to see replicated everywhere—though a court struck down the law. Today forty-three states have at least one municipality with living-wage legislation on the books, or proposed laws.

The movement owes much of its success to the model campaign—exportable anywhere, anytime, fast—that its proponents, above all ACORN's national living-wage center, have created. The prospective living-wage activist can find everything he needs to know in a step-by-step manual, concocted by ACORN director of living-wage campaigns Jed Kern and Wayne State University labor economist David Reynolds.

The manual echoes the organizational theories of legendary radical Saul Alinsky. Coalition building is key. Alinsky's modus operandi was to get diverse constituencies to support his various causes by emphasizing their shared interests. In the same way, ACORN urges local living-wage campaigns to build powerful coalitions of Hispanic workers, inner-city ministers, and various community advocacy groups.

To pull off such coalition building in practice, you need more than a manual, of course; you need money—and the movement has lots of it, thanks to the backing of leftist foundations. The Tides Foundation (which lent financial support to groups opposing the war in Iraq) has given hundreds of thousands of dollars to local and national living-wage groups. The Ford Foundation has been another big contributor.

The coalitions the movement has assembled have included hundreds of religious groups, allowing organizers to present their economic agenda as deeply moral—even divinely sanctioned. Labor groups have signed on too, and some sixty coalitions of labor and interfaith religious groups have sprung up nationally since the mid-1990s to campaign for the living wage.

The Los Angeles–based Clergy and Laity United for Economic Justice (CLUE) is a prominent example. Formed during a successful living-wage campaign in Los Angeles, CLUE brought together an Episcopal priest who had worked to unionize Santa Monica's hotels, a Baptist minister who had once invited a union local into Sunday services to get signatures for a hospital unionizing drive, and a rabbi who had campaigned against the Hollywood stereotyping of Palestinians as terrorists. To highlight the plight of "exploited" hotel service workers deprived of the living wage, the religious trio staged a dramatic procession through Beverly Hills to deposit bitter herbs at the doorstep of the Summit Hotel—evoking the Jewish tradition of using such herbs to recall the Israelites' deliverance from Egyptian bondage.

CLUE is only one of countless examples of the living-wage movement using religion to give it moral clout—in Providence, Rhode Island, churches even held a "living-wage Sunday." "It makes it hard to sound negative about a living-wage campaign when it's presented in those terms," says

Jeffrey Hunter, a former government-affairs specialist with the Detroit Regional Chamber of Commerce, which fought in vain against one of the nation's earliest living-wage laws. Indeed, the very notion of a "living" wage makes anyone who opposes it seem like . . . well, an executioner.

Living-wage campaigns have repeatedly outflanked the business community by practicing what ACORN calls "legislative outmaneuver." Local groups work behind the scenes for months before going public. They draft partisan economists to release timely studies on the prospective benefits of the living wage before opponents can come up with any countering data, and they try to keep any actual legislation off the table until the very last minute, so that there's no fixed target for opponents to get a bead on. ACORN rationalizes these stealth campaigns by arguing that the business community will use, in the words of Kern and Reynolds's organizing manual, a "bag of dirty tricks" to fight the legislation. ACORN ominously—and ludicrously—warns: "Many companies today engage in tactics which hark back to the bloody [unionizing] battles of the 1930s."

ACORN's stealth tactics worked particularly well in Detroit. The Motor City business community had no idea that a living-wage ordinance was about to wallop them until just weeks before it showed up on a citywide referendum. "The organizers won," a labor newsletter observed, "by slipping quietly under Detroit's corporate and political radar." Same story in Boston: "The living-wage ordinance wasn't picked up on the radar until it was too late," complained a local business publication. The Boston law, the publication adds, "initially looked and sounded like yet another innocuous piece of feel-good legislation," but its small print included onerous provisions that required city contractors to work

26

under the supervision of a living-wage enforcement committee and to favor Boston residents for jobs over applicants from beyond the city limits.

These stealth campaigns can produce legislation so bad that it turns even earlier supporters of the living wage into enemies. In Detroit, then-mayor Dennis Archer, initially an ally of the living-wage proposal, excoriated its backers after it became law, because they "did not consult with business or with the [Detroit Regional] Chamber, [so that] the ordinance unfairly impacts on small business and non-profit groups." One hard-hit nonprofit, the Southeastern Michigan Salvation Army, chose not to renew several city contracts to provide housing services to the poor because the living wage raised its costs too high. "We had a good working relationship with the city, but we ended that," says a spokesman. ACORN has since accused the Salvation Army— the *Salvation Army*—of "the big lie" for opposing its living-wage agenda.

Providing the intellectual muscle (such as it is) for the living-wage movement is a small group of Marxoid economists, led by University of Massachusetts–Amherst professor Robert Pollin, a longtime board member of the Union of Radical Political Economists, founded in the 1960s to bring Marxist economics to American universities. Pollin, a New School Ph.D., began serving as an adviser to living-wage campaigns in the mid-1990s, and in 1998 he co-authored (with Stephanie Luce) the book that has become the movement's bible, *The Living Wage: Building a Fair Economy*.

In *The Living Wage*, the class war rages on—and on. Businesses, assert Pollin and Luce, have grown increasingly hostile toward workers in recent years. Their sole evidence for this claim—that the unionization rate has plummeted over the last three decades—ignores the conventional explanations for union decline in the United States: more intense global competition, the shift to a service-oriented, knowledge-based economy, and more generous benefits at nonunionized companies. But never mind: to keep the ravenous capitalists under control, they argue, government clearly needs to impose a national living wage on the private sector. And that's just the beginning. Caps on profits, mandated benefits, rules to make unionization easier, massive taxation—government will manage the economy from top to bottom in *The Living Wage*'s warmed-over socialism.

Indeed, for Pollin and Luce only one economic goal ultimately matters: raising worker salaries—no matter what the cost to the broader economy. Consider their discussion of prevailing wage laws, which set pay rates for public-sector construction projects. Pollin and Luce argue that these laws show what good living-wage legislation will achieve—and what damage the absence of government economic control inflicts on workers. The authors cite a study of nine states that repealed prevailing wage laws and then watched construction-worker annual salaries fall $1,500, or 6 percent. To the authors this is entirely bad news. Nowhere do they try to estimate the savings for government (and thus for taxpayers) once the laws stopped demanding artificially high wages for construction contracts. Nor are the authors interested in the productivity gains for the construction industry—and hence for the economy as a whole—when wages settle at levels dictated by supply and demand, not government bureaucrats.

The complete rejection of a free-market economy by these living-wage gurus—and by the living-wage movement itself—is too much even for many liberal economists. One of the most telling critiques of *The Living Wage* came from self-professed liberal economist and *New York Times* columnist Paul Krugman. In an article archived on the "cranks" section of his website, Krugman observes that "what the living wage is really about is not living standards, or even economics, but morality. Its advocates are basically opposed to the idea that wages are a market price—determined by supply and demand."

But then, if living-wage advocates truly understood the free market, they'd know that ultimately it is far more moral than the centrally controlled economic system they endorse. If there's one thing that the last fifty years tell us, it's that the free market provides far greater economic opportunity and a decent standard of living for far more people than government-controlled markets. Pollin and Luce charge that the American economy is failing because poverty levels in the United States aren't declining significantly. But the authors disregard the effect on the poverty level of the vast stream of immigrants—many of them poor and without skills—cascading into the country every year. What was remarkable about the American economy during the 1990s, when about 13 million low-skilled, low-wage immigrants arrived, is that poverty rates didn't soar, and actually declined slightly—showing the muscularity of our economy in lifting even many of these newcomers out of poverty. A recent Sphere Institute study of low-wage workers in California found that more than 88 percent moved up the economic ladder during the 1990s, their average income more than doubling, to $27,194. If that's not economic justice, nothing is. As for those Pollin (following the Census Bureau) calls "poor": 40 percent own homes, 97 percent own color televisions, two-thirds have air conditioning, and about seven in ten own cars. This is hardly the poverty of a Vietnamese peasant or a 1930s sharecropper.

What's most appalling about Pollin and Luce's economic theorizing, however, is the cavalier way they talk about confiscating income from middle-income Americans to pay for their living-wage scheme. In a follow-up article to his book, published in *The Nation* magazine, Pollin proposed a national living wage of $7.25 per hour, more than $2 above the current minimum. To achieve this, he says, would require a redistribution of income "equal to a reduction of only 6.6 percent in the incomes of the richest 20 percent of households, from roughly $106,600 to $100,000." Only 6.6 percent? Stripping $6,600 a year away from a family making $106,000 a year—a construction worker married to a secretary might well earn this much—is no insignificant levy (even though Pollin's math is wrong). Down more than $550 a month, such a middle-class family might have to forgo sending one of their kids to parochial school, or put off adding a room onto the house for the new baby—goals they may have worked very hard to achieve.

Not only is Pollin's national living wage wildly unfair; it wouldn't work. Numerous studies show that increasing the minimum wage produces no significant reduction in poverty levels and may even increase the number of families living in poverty by eliminating many low-wage jobs. A Congressional Budget Office report, for example, estimates that raising the minimum wage to $6.65 an hour (40 percent less than Pollin's proposal) would eradicate between 200,000 and 600,000 jobs. Moreover it would wreak economic havoc, costing employers $7 billion a year in additional payroll costs. Nor, it's important to add, are minimum-wage earners necessarily struggling economically in the first place. About 64 percent of those receiving the minimum wage today aren't heads of households or sole earners. Many are children still living at home or second wage earners in their family. The average annual household income of a minimum-wage worker in the United States is nearly $44,000. And, of course, almost no workers stay at the minimum for long.

Understandably, given these considerations, most economists today favor earned-income tax credits, not government-mandated wages, as a more effective way to aid the working poor. These tax credits, applied for when filing, provide thousands of dollars in cash rebates from federal and state governments, supplementing the income of low-wage workers without imposing direct new costs on businesses.

Pollin and his radical economist colleagues have regularly descended from the ivory tower to try to convince local elected officials around the country that living-wage laws will help low-wage workers without destroying jobs or significantly raising government expenses. In a 1997 study on a proposed living-wage law in Los Angeles, for instance, Pollin claimed that the legislation—doubling the minimum wage for government contractors—would increase the city's contracting costs by only $7.5 million. The wage hike, Pollin argued, would require just a $40 million increase in contractors' payrolls—something they could easily absorb, he held, given their total sales of $4 billion; little, if any, of the additional cost would be passed on to government.

In a later city-commissioned report, UCLA economist Richard Sander—who calls himself a "progressive Democrat" and a defender of narrowly drawn living-wage laws—demolished Pollin's rosy scenario. Sander estimated that the actual cost of the legislation to city government would be $42 million—six times Pollin's estimate. Moreover, Sander noted, adding $42 million to firms' salary costs, as the law proposed, was nothing to sneeze at—as is evident as soon as you compare the new costs not with companies' total revenues, as Pollin did, but with their very much smaller profits.

Los Angeles eventually enacted narrower living-wage legislation, and Sander has completed a study of it. He found that the city, and not its contractors, is bearing all the cost of its living wage. Hit with the legislation, Los Angeles vendors either raised prices or reduced services to the city. Adding in the expense of monitoring compliance with the law, the city bears "more than 100 percent of the cost," Sander says.

Joining the radical economists on the front lines of living-wage campaigns are the unions, which have their own reasons for supporting the legislation. For unions and their political allies, the threat of the living wage has become a powerful means to pressure firms to unionize. About two dozen current living-wage ordinances specifically exempt unionized companies from the legislation. So if a local city contractor paying two dollars below the living wage unionizes, it won't have to raise salaries—at least in the short term.

No wonder that many living-wage campaigns erupt in places where unions are fighting tough organizing battles with local businesses. In Santa Monica, for example, a living-wage campaign got under way after a local hotel union had failed in a three-year effort to organize workers in the city's tourism district. The living-wage legislation that Santa Monica's left-leaning city council then crafted and passed, with heavy union input all down the line, subjected every business in the tourism district to its terms—except unionized hotels. Santa Monica voters eventually over-turned the law in a referendum.

These kinds of union-tailored living-wage laws are so blatantly pro-labor that they may be illegal. When a law forces employers to choose between paying higher wages and accepting a union, says Atlanta labor lawyer Arch Stokes, it amounts to a collective-bargaining ordinance. Municipalities don't have the legal right to supersede federal labor law and pass such legislation.

Municipal unions like living-wage laws too, for a different reason. By raising the cost of city contracts, these laws make privatization efforts less appealing and thus protect the jobs of city workers. After all, if cities can't save much money by contracting out work traditionally done by high-paid municipal workers, what is the point of privatizing? ACORN puts it bluntly in its manual: "The Living Wage undercuts the incentive to privatize."

Ironically, even as ACORN battles to make businesses and nonprofit contractors pay higher wages, the State of California has sued the group for paying its own workers below the minimum wage. ACORN argued that minimum-wage laws infringe on the group's First Amendment right of free speech. If it had to pay the minimum wage, the organization says—shamelessly echoing the arguments of the businesses it is forever seeking to regulate—it would have to hire fewer people, making it harder to get its message out.

This kind of hypocrisy is typical of ACORN and indeed of the New New Left in general. The nation's largest radical organization, with 120,000 dues-paying members in 700 poor neighborhoods, ACORN promotes itself as standing "virtually alone in its dedication to organizing the poor and powerless." But often what ACORN actually promotes are policies that help it expand its own programs and power, or advance the interests of its public-sector allies, regardless of the impact on the poor. Beyond its living wage campaigns, for instance, ACORN has led many anti-privatization fights, including a successful battle in 2001 to derail former New York City mayor Rudy Giuliani's effort to hire a private school operator to run five failing public schools. ACORN demonized the company, Edison Schools, carting the New York union movement's trademark giant rat balloon to a noisy rally in front of Edison's Manhattan offices. But in its pursuit of a "voice" for the poor, ACORN has never criticized its allies in the New York City teacher's union as the main cause of the decline of the city's schools—a decline that harms the urban poor tragically. After all, ACORN is itself part of the failed system it was protecting: it uses foundation grants to operate public schools in New York under a Board of Education program that permits community-based organizations to do so.

ACORN is nothing if not opportunistic in exploiting its role as defender of the poor. The organization has emerged a leading manipulator of the Community Reinvestment Act, the federal law that requires banks to invest a certain percentage of their capital in poorer neighborhoods. Although researchers find little discrimination these days in bank lending, banks typically "hire" ACORN as a consultant on CRA matters, not surprising when you consider that the group has made its reputation filing CRA complaints to derail bank mergers. Thus, when J. P. Morgan and Chase Manhattan wanted to merge, both banks separately "donated" hundreds of thousands of dollars to ACORN. "The same corporations that pay ransom to Jesse Jackson and Al Sharpton pay ransom to ACORN," says Robert L. Woodson, president of the National Center for Neighborhood Enterprise, a Washington, D.C.–based group that provides training to leaders of community-based organizations.

With ACORN in the lead, the living-wage movement's next steps are clear—and potentially devastating to urban prosperity. Activists are working hard to expand the number of those covered by existing living-wage legislation. In New York City, one of the first places to enact a living-wage law, the new city council and Mayor Bloomberg extended it to fifty thousand or so privately employed health-care workers. The powerful Local 1199, representing some home health-care workers who fall under the extended legislation, lobbied heavily for the change. Thanks to Mayor Bloomberg, New York will now have the largest number of workers covered by any living-wage law in the nation. Other cities have expanded their laws too. Oakland's initial edict, to take just one example, originally applied only to city contracts, but in early 2002 city lawmakers extended it to firms in the government-subsidized Port of Oakland.

It's not just the number of those covered that the movement wants to expand. ACORN activists have begun advocating more capacious living-wage laws that incorporate affirmative-action requirements, restrictions on employers' use of part-time workers, mandatory vacation time, and prohibitions on using revenues from public contracts to hire law firms to resist union-organizing efforts. San Francisco, already moving in this direction, amended its law a year after it passed to include certain health-care benefits on top of the wage boost.

As living-wage laws get broader and more expansive, supporters are also trying to offload some of the cost, increasingly burdensome to cities, onto state and federal governments. The revision of the New York City law, for instance, zeroed in on health-care workers because many of them work in state-funded programs. City council members who sponsored the legislation justified it by saying that the state's share of the cost would be five or six times higher than the city's. And Detroit's law included contracts that the city simply administered but that were paid for by federal agencies, such as Housing and Urban Development.

Emboldened by their successes, living-wage advocates have gone on to help organize local coalitions to lobby for much broader left-wing economic programs, under the slogan "sustainable economics." ACORN's own organizing manual says it best: "[A]cross the country grassroots projects are using Living Wage as a campaign tool for building broad and comprehensive progressive agendas."

Sustainable economics covers a whole agenda of government social and fiscal policies to redistribute income and regulate business that add up to socialism by another name. The Milwaukee coalition responsible for that city's living-wage law, for example, has pushed for an economic-development plan that includes more money for community job-training programs, laws that bolster union organizing and that require "socially responsible banking," government investment to create "environmentally friendly" jobs—and on and on. Its agenda even leaps beyond economics to require multicultural public-school curricula, more ethnically diverse teaching staffs, and greater inclusion in curricula of topics such as workers' rights, the history of the labor movement, and family leave laws.

Lest this grand program sound like mere pie in the sky, note that living-wage advocates in California have already succeeded in getting the state's assembly to pass a sustainable economic plan for the greater Sacramento area. Startlingly, this plan would force growing suburban communities to share tax income with the city, and it restricts suburban growth, so that residents and businesses will find it more difficult to move just outside the city limits. Having created the policies on taxation, crime, and education that propelled the middle class out of urban America in the first place, the left is now looking for a way to slow that flight by governmental fiat. It's yet more bad news for cities—especially since the rest of the country fortunately is still free and has plenty of room.

T W O

· ·

Union U.

Just when you thought America's universities—with their multicultural curricula, anti-Americanism, and intolerance of open debate—couldn't possibly get any more radical and partisan, along comes the next new thing: the labor movement's successful effort to co-opt academic departments and programs on campuses from coast to coast.

For years, universities have offered courses in "labor studies," often taught by ardent labor movement activists. But ever since the mid-1990s, when the labor movement began to revive under the leadership of AFL-CIO chief John Sweeney, these departments have grown in importance, nurtured by a new generation of savvy union leaders. These programs have come to define their mission chiefly as supporting labor and its organizing efforts rather than educating students. Working in close cooperation with unions—and with scant input from anyone who does not follow the labor movement's party line—these programs now pump out one-sided research to bolster labor's legislative agenda, and they dispatch student interns to help unions organize workers. They sponsor seminars and radio programs that advance union goals, and they use classrooms to push the labor movement's tendentious views of privatization, globalization, and corporate America. Even more than other programs in today's increasingly politicized universities, labor studies programs substitute propaganda and activism for the disinterested pursuit of truth.

Who funds this whirlwind of activity that advances the private interests of a small subset of American workers? We, the taxpayers, do: nearly all of these programs, especially the most militant and ideological, operate from publicly funded universities.

When labor studies programs arose just after World War II, mostly in the "extension" or continuing-education divisions of universities, their aim was modest: to help create a better-educated generation of union workers to combat mob control, corruption, and Communist influence. "If labor leaders could be better educated, it was thought this would lead to fewer confrontations and fewer strikes," says Judy Ancel, director of the Institute for Labor Studies at the University of Missouri–Kansas City. At first, labor viewed these programs with suspicion and seemed doubtful that the handful of innocuous courses on how to run union meetings and elections, for instance, or on the duties of a shop steward, workplace safety, and contract administration, could help them much.

But this modest field began to change rapidly in the late 1960s, when state legislatures started giving public-sector employees the right to organize. Newly potent public unions, in their quest for an ever greater share of taxpayer spending, advocated for more labor-related studies resources at public universities (among many other things). In quick order, many states complied, setting up labor studies courses, undergraduate majors, and research centers on labor topics, until by the mid-1970s several dozen centers and departments were flourishing, mostly at public institutions. They arose just as a new generation of administrators and professors began to radicalize instruction by dumping core curriculum requirements, lowering standards, and replacing the objective pursuit of knowledge with social agendas. The result was a new kind of labor studies, more apt to encourage activism than to teach students the fine points of employment trends or labor law. And these programs defined "labor" almost exclusively as "organized labor."

The nearly fifty such programs operating today pulsate with energy and churn out new initiatives. In 1995, for example, the University of Massachusetts at Amherst began a labor studies M.A. program in union leadership and administration—in essence, a professional school for union leaders that is emblematic of the transformation of the field from a backwater of continuing education to postgraduate academic status. In Michigan, in the late 1990s, the labor center at publicly funded Wayne State University, working with the radical left-wing group ACORN, began providing technical support to living-wage campaigns around the country. The center produced a detailed manual on how to organize such campaigns, which helped spark successful efforts to raise the minimum wage for some workers in dozens of cities and provided a model of how academics could decisively advance union causes. In 2001 the California legislature, in response to union lobbying, dedicated millions in state money for research on labor issues and for a new multicampus center for working-class studies that churns out reports supporting labor's positions on a variety of subjects.

Labor leaders have forged close alliances with these university programs, using union resources to cultivate students, professors, and administrators. AFL-CIO boss Sweeney quickly recognized that today's left-wing university could provide labor with a new set of allies. Observing the fervor with which students and professors often supported university cafeteria and maintenance employees' bids for higher wages, Sweeney moved to exploit the momentum.

In 1996 he began a union-funded program called "Union Summer," in which college students spend five weeks working on union campaigns and learning how to organize. They then take their new skills back to campus as trained activists. These labor interns have helped lead protests on dozens of campuses against the use of low-paid foreign workers to manufacture university T-shirts and sweatshirts. They have marched in support of strikes by university and local government workers, and they have organized protests against cuts in state university budgets. More than 2,300 students have gone through the program to date.

Cementing the strong ties that labor has built to labor studies professors and administrators, the scholarly association that represents labor studies programs merged with a Communications Workers of America local in 2000, making this scholarly organization in effect an AFL-CIO affiliate. The new organization, the United Association for Labor Education, now holds its annual "education" conference in conjunction with the AFL-CIO. The theme of one recent conference: "Building a Strong Grassroots Union Movement." Educators participated in such workshops as "Grassroots Strategies to Support Labor's Political Agenda" and "Organizing Strategies for an Ever-Changing Work-force." Only a very few panels, such as one on teaching ethics in labor education classes, bore any relation to ped-agogy. Thus have university professors been drafted as ad-vocates for the union movement.

Although multicultural and other radical agendas have politicized course offerings in many university depart-ments, labor studies is emerging as among the most parti-san of fields because of the close bonds between unions and academics. Today many labor studies programs state plainly that they exist primarily to promote unions and cre-ate a generation of advocates and activists. Their mission statements read like political manifestos rather than educa-tional credos. Wayne State University's labor center de-clares its main goal is "strengthening the capacity of organized labor to represent the needs and interests of workers" in a world of "corporate elites or state power." The labor program at the University of California at Berkeley aims "to support the labor movement by providing research and education." The University of Massachusetts–Amherst says it trains students for a life in "organizations advocat-ing for workers' rights."

This emphasis on advocacy has turned the classroom into a soapbox, from which professors rail against what la-bor considers its biggest threats. Enemy Number One is privatization, the practice by which governments contract with private companies to perform services—from running school cafeterias to picking up trash—usually done by unionized government employees. Although many urban reformers view privatization as an important way for gov-ernment to spur efficiencies and save taxpayers money, a course in the University of Illinois at Urbana's labor studies program demonizes privatization as nothing more than the "efforts of market-oriented forces to auction off public services to the highest bidder" (though usually such contracts go to the lowest bidder). According to the course description, students will learn that privatization's nefarious purpose is to "dispense political patronage and to destroy public sector unions."

Similarly, labor studies professors teach students that corporations are invariably evil empires to be battled. Declaring that we live in "an era of crushing corporate power and aggressive opposition to unions," for example, a course in the master's program at UMass Amherst teaches students how to do "corporate research," examining firms for facts that unions can use to embarrass them or to gain political leverage over them in organizing campaigns or contract negotiations. In the same spirit, the UMass Amherst program sees financiers as a similarly vast and powerful conspiracy. The course description for "Labor in the U.S. Economy" includes a segment called "Finance Capital's Control of National and Corporate Governance" and, as an antidote, another segment entitled "Reclaiming Our Economy: Common Sense Strategies for Workers," based on AFL-CIO curriculum materials.

Little wonder that the labor movement is thrilled with today's labor studies programs and that AFL-CIO's Sweeney heaps praise on the UMass Amherst program. "The Labor Center," he enthuses, "has provided unflinching support for the labor movement through their research and teaching." Of course, only the tendentious world of modern academia would view such an endorsement as meritorious or would consider such partisan classes higher education. "There is no analogy to this kind of partisanship," says the historian

Howard Dickman, author of *Industrial Democracy in America*. "Imagine a business school that taught union-busting skills in its human resource classes and helped local businesses fight unions as part of a class project."

With their sharp leftward tilt, many labor studies programs are housed not in business administration or economics departments, which generally demand peer-reviewed faculty research and try to balance points of view in their courses, but in urban studies or interdisciplinary social sciences departments, where less rigorous standards of scholarship and more overt politicization of instruction often reign. More and more labor studies departments are interdisciplinary programs, with course options far afield from the study of labor markets, human resources, or workplace safety. Students in the University of Michigan's undergraduate labor studies program get to pick from courses like "Colonialism and Globalization," "Gender, Development, and Inequality," and "Race, Gender, and Empire in the Nuclear Age." There is no mistaking the slant in these courses. "Gender and Globalization," for instance, is "a critical and feminist examination of globalization," its professor writes.

One current university trend that labor studies programs have enthusiastically embraced is "service learning," which emphasizes community activism and political organizing as integral to the curriculum. Typical is the labor studies program at UMass Boston, housed in the school's College of Public and Community Service, where "students are encouraged to become socially and politically active." At Queens College of the City University of New York, professors developed a labor internship program, the Solidarity Project, with help from the university's Education Center for Community Organizing, whose purpose is to stimulate social activism and community organizing in students. So pervasive has the culture of service learning become that administrators now regularly praise student activists who oppose their own campus policies. "We look at student protests as being a normal part of the educational process," one of Harvard's lawyers told the press, after students protested a university labor policy.

This elevation of activism as central to the educational experience has provided labor studies programs with a rationale for establishing numerous internship programs that send students out to battle for labor against the interests of businesses and taxpayers. Interns at UCLA's labor program, attracted by the slogan "If you are passionate about social and economic change, apply for the Summer Internship Program," have helped unionize janitorial workers and have campaigned for controversial legislation to force Santa Monica businesses, including many small retailers, to raise the salaries of some employees. Interns from Berkeley's labor center have worked on similar living-wage campaigns in Oakland and San Francisco. On the East Coast, UMass Amherst's intern program has supplied student organizers for campaigns to unionize Georgia garment workers and Bay State nurses.

Parents and taxpayers don't necessarily share the academics' enthusiasm for such programs. Nic Ramos, who reports that in UCLA's labor internship program he "learned everything from labor organizing, Gender Justice, Racial Justice, Queer Rights, Environmental Justice—I mean just everything and anything there was critical to studies of American life today," also notes that his immigrant parents are "wary of my involvement in such political activities." And businessman Marvin Zeidler, co-owner of the Broadway

Deli in Santa Monica and one of the business owners who campaigned against the local living-wage law, was shocked to learn that those out on street corners agitating in favor of the law were fulfilling university requirements. "I had no idea they used students," he says. "As a taxpayer in California, I am funding the UC system. This is not the kind of activity I want to fund."

Perhaps academe's most important weapons in support of union causes are the reports that labor centers industriously churn out on subjects key to the labor movement's legislative agenda, especially free trade, globalization, living-wage legislation, and poverty. These reports, with their veneer of academic objectivity, appear to provide scholarly, objective, scientific proof of labor's most cherished contentions. But the reports, rarely dispatched to peer-reviewed journals, are mere propaganda. To read these "studies," touted in the press as nonpartisan, is to realize just how endangered in today's university are such notions as disinterested scholarship and inquiry after the truth.

For example, when nonprofit social services groups in Detroit complained that the city's new living-wage law forced them to raise salaries and cut services, Wayne State University's labor center rushed out a study claiming that the law had little impact on such organizations—though subsequently one of the area's key nonprofits, the Salvation Army, withdrew from several contracts with the city of Detroit because of the law. The study became a powerful tool for advocates in other cities considering living-wage legislation to raise the minimum pay of workers in companies with city contracts. A *Pittsburgh Post-Gazette* columnist reported that fears that a proposed local law would harm nonprofits were overblown; after all, "[d]espite the same dire predictions by opponents that Detroit's living-wage law would force nonprofits to close or curtail services and cause layoffs, the [Wayne State] study found that only 20 percent of the nonprofits faced significant financial obstacles." The story not only failed to mention the experience of the Salvation Army but also neglected to point out that Wayne State's labor studies program is closely aligned with the living-wage movement, that the department acknowledges providing "direct technical support" to living-wage campaigns, and that one of the authors of the Detroit study, David Reynolds, is a former union organizer and co-author of a guide on how to mount successful campaigns to pass living-wage legislation.

Nevertheless, labor-friendly politicians regularly invoke the academic authority of these reports. During debates over San Francisco's living-wage laws, the president of the city's board of supervisors—the law's chief proponent—touted a UC Berkeley study claiming that the proposed law would have little financial impact on the economy or municipal government. The Berkeley department that sponsored the study, the Institute of Industrial Relations, is a labor-friendly entity whose official list of living-wage "resources" for Californians mentions only groups that support living-wage laws; the report's author is a member of a group of radical political economists whose theories are far outside the free-market mainstream. A later, nonpartisan study, commissioned by the San Francisco City Council and conducted by economists from San Francisco State University, concluded that the proposed law would cost vastly more than the UC Berkeley study estimated.

Not only tendentious, these reports often trample on even more basic rules of scholarship, including the prohibition against presenting someone else's work as your own. As the business-backed Employment Policies Institute points out, not only do dozens of studies on the living wage's effects in cities around the country reach the same conclusions; many use virtually the same language. A study by Florida International University's labor center argues that living-wage laws make businesses better performers because higher salaries attract and retain better workers. "One would expect county contractors, after passage of a living-wage ordinance, to become the 'Cadillac' firms in their industries," the study says. In strikingly similar terms, a Wayne State report on the subject says: "It would be expected the living wage law would encourage contractors and firms using city financial assistance to become the premier firms in their industries." And then both reports go on to say, in the exact same language: "They should attract and keep the best workers, have the most productive workforce and, over time, deliver the highest quality of services." In the academia of yore, such borrowing of judgments, ideas, and language without direct attribution could doom a scholar's career.

And yet, incredibly, what passes for scholarly research in labor studies programs can get even shoddier than this. Out of some $6 million that the state legislature allocated to the University of California's Institute for Labor and Employment for research on working-class issues, $12,000 went to finance the training of local union workers to create "dossiers of data on major property owners and investors" to fight gentrification and "slumlordism"; $25,000 went to a study "to develop models for mobilizing and organizing" young workers; $15,000 went to a study of campaigns that successfully fight privatization of welfare services; and $7,000 went to study how unions are fighting the effects of globalization in California's ports. Concludes George Mason University economics professor James Bennett, editor of the *Journal of Labor Research*: "There's no way you can legitimately call union organizing 'research.'"

Not that labor studies programs are shy about dropping the mask of scholarship and engaging in propaganda, pure and simple. The labor program at UMass Lowell, for instance, uses its website to disseminate "action alerts" about local union campaigns, warning that a union local is under attack from a movie theater chain or imploring readers to assist an organizing effort at a local supermarket chain by downloading a form letter to send to the chain's president. The labor studies program at the University of Missouri–Kansas City sponsors intensely partisan radio programs, dubbed *Heartland Labor Forum*. Billed as examinations of workplace and economic issues, the incendiary shows, prepared by local union members, bear titles like: "Speak Out on Corporate Greed," "The New Tyranny of George III: Union Busting Executive Orders," and "Privatization: Will Bush Open the Floodgates?"

It's easy to view what has happened at labor studies programs as simply one more manifestation of disturbing trends within the larger academy over the last few decades: the victory of advocacy over the disinterested pursuit of knowledge, the abandoning of standards, the ascendance of race and gender politics, the growth of anti-Americanism. And, giving credence to that idea, labor studies programs, from CUNY's Queens College to UMass Boston to Washington State's Evergreen State College, took a highly conspicuous role in leading campus opposition to the recent war in Iraq.

But something also sets the labor studies phenomenon apart from the campuswide culture wars. Unlike gender studies or race studies, labor studies undeviatingly promotes the interests of a remarkably tiny constituency: the union movement, representing a minuscule 13 percent of America's private-sector workers and about 35 percent of public employees. It's an amazing coup for organized labor and its allies to have tapped so brilliantly into the campus culture wars for their own narrow purposes. Set amid the larger battles within universities, it's a coup that also has gone largely unnoticed by traditional academics, businesses, the media, and the taxpayers whose dollars support this agenda.

Back in the sixties and seventies, when labor bosses were culturally conservative, supported pro-growth policies, and sent their hardhats to battle long-haired students over the war in Vietnam, who would ever have thought that the day would come when union leaders would co-opt the professors?

THREE

· ·

Why Wal-Mart Is the Enemy

Here's a story you're unlikely to read in the spate of press attacks on Wal-Mart these days:

When Hartford, Connecticut, tore down a blighted housing project, city officials hatched an innovative plan to redevelop the land: lure Wal-Mart there, entice other retailers with the promise of being near the discount giant, and then use the development's revenues to build new housing. Wal-Mart, after some convincing, agreed, and city officials and neighborhood residents celebrated a big win—better shopping, more jobs, and new housing in one of America's poorest cities.

But then, out of nowhere, outsiders claiming to represent the local community began protesting. Astonished city leaders and local residents quickly discovered the forces fueling the campaign: a Connecticut chapter of the United Food and Commercial Workers Union; and ACORN, the radical community group. Outraged residents fought back, denouncing outside interference, but opponents persisted, filing three separate lawsuits that have delayed construction, including a ludicrous suit claiming that the development would destroy unique vegetation that has sprouted since the housing project came down. "These people looked for every possible reason to stop a project that the community wants," says Jackie Fongemie, a frustrated community activist who has fought for the store. "Where were the environmentalists when rats were running wild around this place?"

Although Wal-Mart has encountered opposition for years from anti-sprawl activists or small-town merchants worried about the competition, the Hartford drama exemplifies a brand-new kind of opposition, a coordinated effort in which unions, activist groups like ACORN and the National Organization for Women, environmentalist groups, private- and public-sector unions, and even plaintiffs' attorneys work together in effective alliances. They are fighting the giant retailer not only store by store but in statehouses, city halls, and courts. They even managed to make Wal-Mart an issue in the 2004 presidential campaign: several Democratic hopefuls indicted the American shopper's favorite store as unfriendly to working people.

This new war on Wal-Mart is more than just a skirmish over store sites or union-organizing efforts. It is an attack on a company that embodies the dynamic, productivity-driven, customer-oriented U.S. economy that emerged in the 1990s by opponents who advocate a different economics. Arguing that there is a hidden cost to business's increasing emphasis on low prices and high employee output, these opponents seek government edicts to force Wal-Mart and discounters like it to raise wages and offer workers more benefits. Wal-Mart's opponents are rushing into battle just as the company and some of its imitators are expanding their brand of retailing to many underserved urban communities starved for the low prices, broad selection, and friendly service these stores offer, making the conflict a vital issue not just in Wal-Mart's traditional rural and suburban markets but, increasingly, in American cities.

When Sam Walton started out as a retail entrepreneur in the 1940s, few could have dreamed that he would hatch anything that would become so successful—or controversial. A World War II vet who had worked as a clerk in J. C. Penney stores, Walton started modestly by buying an old Ben Franklin 5&10 in the tiny town of Newton, Arkansas, population seven thousand. When his landlord wouldn't renew his lease, he headed to even smaller Bentonville, Arkansas—population five thousand—where he opened another variety store and then started building ever larger ones in nearby towns. A conservative on family, religious, and civic issues, Walton was a radical in business, discontented with old-fashioned country retailing. After studying such discount pioneers as the E. J. Korvette chain in New York and New Jersey, Walton opened his first Wal-Mart Discount City on July 2, 1962, in Rogers, Arkansas.

Although his first Wal-Marts were chaotic, with goods piled high on tables, the stores charged unprecedentedly low prices, and crowds flocked to them, some traveling hundreds of miles to shop. One time, the local fire department had to be called to a store opening to control the mob. Recognizing that he had something unique to offer, Walton expanded his idea, so that by 1970, when he offered Wal-Mart stock on Wall Street, the company already boasted thirty-two stores and $31 million in annual revenues. Then

Wal-Mart grew even more rapidly, to seventy-eight stores and $168 million in revenues in 1974, and to over $1 billion in sales by 1980. Not Arab oil embargoes, interest-rate spikes, or recessions could stop the company's growth, and its stock soared, growing and splitting four times during its first ten years, so that by 1980 an investment of $1,650 in one hundred shares at the initial public offering had already grown to $80,000—all during a period when the Dow Jones average barely budged.

Despite its acclaim from rural shoppers and a small circle of investors, Wal-Mart largely flew below the radar screen during its earliest years. The few small-town merchants and their political allies who protested that the stores were destroying town shopping districts sensed, though they didn't completely understand it at the time, that Wal-Mart was at the forefront of a revolution that would transform the American landscape. Consumers were abandoning small, inefficient Main Street stores to shop in expansive shopping centers offering everything at one stop and at low prices. Before Wal-Mart, general-merchandise stores typically operated on profit margins as high as 45 percent of sales, but Wal-Mart managed on an operating profit of just 22 percent and passed the difference on to customers, who flocked in when they saw how much they could save. Merchants predicted that Wal-Mart would hike its prices as soon as the competition disappeared, but years later Wal-Mart is still considered among the sharpest-priced, best-value retailers in the world—even in its original small-town markets.

Walton figured out that one key to success was to develop a corporate culture in which management and employees worked together with the sole aim of serving the customer, a revolutionary idea at the time, though now a standard management technique. In his biography, Walton wrote that he feared a unionized Wal-Mart would never develop such a culture, because unions depended on driving a wedge between management and employees, "and divisiveness, by breaking down direct communication, makes it harder to take care of customers, to be competitive, and to gain market share." Early in its history, Wal-Mart fought a few tough battles to stay nonunion; once, when the Teamsters tried to organize a distribution center, employees showed up for work to find a ninety-foot-long wall tacked with newspaper stories about Teamsters violence and corruption—and the mysterious, mob-related disappearance of union boss Jimmy Hoffa.

But Wal-Mart also staved off unions with another then revolutionary and now standard management technique: giving employees a stake in the company's success, offering them one of the earliest profit-sharing programs, which, as an incentive to work hard, doled out shares in one of the best-performing stocks of the last fifty years. In his biography, Walton tells of hourly employees who prospered, like truck driver Bob Clark, who accumulated more than $700,000 in his profit-sharing account over twenty years; and Jean Kelley, a shipping supervisor who in ten years at Wal-Mart accrued nearly $230,000 in Wal-Mart shares.

Although it's been more than a decade since Walton died, the company's success still rests on "Mr. Sam's" formula. From its earliest days, while Wal-Mart scoured the marketplace for the best prices on everything from Crest toothpaste to power drills to girls' dresses, it also kept a relentlessly tight rein on expenses, as executives bunked together on buying trips and passed up gifts like Super Bowl tickets or lavish dinners from suppliers, because those perks ultimately drove up the price of goods. Walton shunned fancy headquarters and kept his front office lean and mean, so that the company never spent more than 2 percent of sales on administrative costs, less than half the industry average. "Every time Wal-Mart spends one dollar foolishly, it comes right out of our customers' pockets," Walton once said, and the company still lives by that adage.

The folksy country retailer also quickly recognized the value of efficient inventory and delivery systems, ultimately leading a technology revolution that spread throughout the retailing industry and its chain of suppliers. With its first units in isolated rural markets, Wal-Mart's front office had unusual problems communicating with its stores and getting merchandise to them, so the company experimented early on with new technologies. It was among the first to put computers—and later, scanners—in stores to track inventory, starting back in the 1970s. With information from those computers telling headquarters what consumers were buying and what items needed to be reordered, Wal-Mart managers realized they could revolutionize the way merchandise moved to stores. Instead of building warehouses that stored vast stocks of items, they constructed a network of computerized distribution centers, which on one side received needed goods from suppliers and almost immediately sent them out the other side to individual stores just before the stores ran out of them. The company even added a satellite system that could track its delivery trucks through global positioning technology and tell store managers exactly when shipments would arrive. So efficient did the whole system become that Wal-Mart was soon selling goods in its stores even before it had to pay its suppliers for them, vastly cutting its inventory costs.

Nor did Wal-Mart stop these innovations at its own doorstep. It compelled suppliers to squeeze out their own waste and to connect to its computerized inventory system, so that a factory could know when it was time to stamp out twenty thousand more ten-inch frying pans or fifteen thousand more twelve-inch ones. The ordering, manufacturing, and delivery of products became one seamless process, continually responding to consumer demands, with a minimum of waste. It also spurred a vast boom in technology investments by U.S. retailers, helping produce tens of thousands of high-tech jobs. "I've become a better company dealing with Wal-Mart," says Charlie Woo, chief executive of Megatoys Inc., a Los Angeles manufacturer. "To meet their requests, I constantly have to upgrade my systems and improve my business practices."

Pursuing this formula brilliantly, Wal-Mart has led a productivity revolution in retailing, which has super-charged the American economy, making a vast cornucopia of merchandise affordable to ordinary consumers, thanks to Wal-Mart's much lower prices than in the days when small-town merchants took their 45 percent profit margins. The McKinsey consulting firm best summed up the cumulative impact of the company's influence in a report entitled "The Wal-Mart Effect," which estimates that the retailer's focus on low prices and its constant stream of money-saving innovations accounted for up to one-quarter of the entire U.S. economy's prodigious productivity gains in the 1990s boom—when inflation held steady despite a soaring economy. Savvy investor Warren Buffett even declared that Wal-Mart—not Microsoft or some other technology company—has contributed more than any other business to the health of the U.S. economy.

Because Wal-Mart represents the leading edge of this American business revolution, the left's crusade against it is more than just a battle against a single company. It is instead a clash of worldviews, as unions and their allies, representing a narrow band of special interests masquerading as a populist movement, try to convince the public that super-efficient discounters like Wal-Mart lower workers' standard of living even as they actually raise living standards by offering goods to so many at such low prices.

What moved the battle into high gear was Wal-Mart's mid-1990s push into major cities and suburban areas beyond the culturally more friendly Deep South and Southwest. The company opened stores in politically liberal cities like Los Angeles, Baltimore, and Philadelphia, and even debuted a new "urban prototype" store that presages future openings in the very heart of big cities. At the same time the company perfected its super-centers, which, at about 200,000 square feet, are the size of four football fields and contain as broad an assortment of merchandise and services as one can find under one retail roof. Shoppers line up at a store's digital photo kiosks to order pictures, test out fishing supplies, fill prescriptions in the pharmacy, check out 50-inch projection TVs, shop for steaks or milk in the store's grocery section, and queue up in one of 30 or more checkout lanes.

The grocery departments are at the heart of the battle. They represent a grave new threat to unionized food stores. Although unions have been unable to organize the discount industry—Wal-Mart competitors like Target and Kohl's are also nonunion—they have been much more successful in supermarket chains, so when Wal-Mart began pulverizing the grocery competition with its low prices and vast selection, it threatened union gains. In just ten years Wal-Mart expanded from thirty-four of these hybrid stores to nearly thirteen hundred. In an age when supermarkets already operate on single-digit profit margins, these stores charge a few cents less on staples like toothpaste, soap, and razor blades but can be as much as one-third cheaper on higher-margin items like premium meat and vegetables. As a result, Wal-Mart's entry into a market can still drive down grocery prices 15 percent, and as a result the $250 billion company has already become the country's largest grocer, with a fifth of the market. Some analysts predict that it could eventually capture 35 percent of grocery sales in the United States—a staggering achievement in a business where local tastes and suppliers still matter so much and regional, rather than national, chains predominate.

In response to this success, a coalition of more than 30 unions and left-wing activist groups organized a national day of protest in October 2002, urging shoppers to boycott the company as a "Merchant of Shame." The boycott campaign got no results, but the coalition's legislative battles are another story. California, where Wal-Mart wants to open 40 or so super centers, is the main front in the war. The company is aiming for a 20 percent market share in a state whose supermarket industry is one of the nation's most heavily unionized, with about 250,000 workers under contract. But the anti–Wal-Mart coalition has successfully lobbied more than a dozen cities and towns to pass various kinds of ordinances to keep Wal-Mart out while dozens of other such bills are in the legislative hopper. One in Los Angeles, for instance, would force real-estate developers to conduct time-consuming studies to measure the potential job losses that might result from a new Wal-Mart store.

But the real issue isn't job losses; it is union wages. Unions argue that supermarkets in California typically pay store workers from $18 to $25 an hour (though Wal-Mart says those wages represent the high end of the union scale), while Wal-Mart pays its California store associates about $10 an hour on average. The effect of Wal-Mart entering the market, union advocates say, would be a vast reduction in the wage pool. One study estimates that if Wal-Mart supercenters enter the San Diego area, the competition could drive down grocery wages between $100 million and $200 million annually. "While charging low prices obviously has some consumer benefits . . . these benefits come at a steep price for American workers," charges an anti–Wal-Mart diatribe by California Democratic congressman George Miller. Efforts by Wal-Mart and others to control costs are "short-sighted strategies" that "ultimately undermine our economy" by lowering living standards, Miller's report claims.

Union-supported policy groups, like the San Diego–based Center on Policy Initiatives, argue that Wal-Mart should be made to pay "sustainable" or "self-sufficiency" wages—wages that they deem adequate to meet basic needs—in order to gain permission to expand in California. The "sustainable" wage has become a popular idea with the left, which argues that minimum wages should be much higher than the federal $5.15 per hour and should be based on an area's cost of living. In many parts of California, liberal economists estimate, that means up to $38,000 a year for an adult worker supporting a spouse.

But the left's case ignores the greater benefit that an efficient operator like Wal-Mart brings to shoppers and an entire economy by driving down prices and forcing other stores to perform better. A Wal-Mart–sponsored study, undertaken by the Los Angeles County Economic Development Corporation, estimates that Wal-Mart's entry into the local market would save county shoppers about $1.78 billion annually and southern California shoppers $3.76 billion annually, or nearly $600 per household. Shoppers would redirect those savings, the LAEDC says, into other uses that could create up to 36,000 new jobs, more than offsetting the estimated loss of 3,000 to 5,000 jobs resulting from a drop in the grocery industry wage pool.

Despite the left's charges that Wal-Mart doesn't pay sustainable wages, the company has little trouble recruiting, in part because the gap between its pay and union wages isn't as large as opponents claim. The LAEDC study calculates that the true difference is less than three dollars an hour, which can be offset by the other benefits that a growing company like Wal-Mart offers workers, especially in the form of advancement and stock benefits. While employment at unionized food stores tends to be static, with union members never moving up from their original jobs and relying on wage increases built into contracts to advance their salaries, Wal-Mart promotes heavily from within. More than two-thirds of its management started out working in its stores.

It was just such opportunity for advancement that motivated Sharie Beck, who took a cashier's job at a new Wal-Mart in a mall in Baldwin Hills, Los Angeles, for a lower salary than she'd been earning elsewhere. "I plan to advance in the company," she told the press about her decision to join Wal-Mart. Other applicants obviously concur, because when it opened one of its first Los Angeles–area stores, in the Panorama City mall, Wal-Mart had seven thousand job applicants during its first week. "The thing about Wal-Mart," says Aaron Rios, a former shelf stocker who is now a district manager, "is that there is a place here for part-time workers who just need to earn some extra money, and also for anyone looking for a career. The company is so big and growing so quickly that you could even change careers and still stay with Wal-Mart."

Regardless of the campaign against it, Wal-Mart is generating enormous support in many of its newest markets, especially in lower-income urban areas where shoppers often have few choices among stores and where prices are typically high—especially for groceries, which account for so big a percentage of low-income budgets. Minority communities traditionally friendly to the left's agenda have shocked opponents by welcoming Wal-Mart and working closely with it. Unions tried to stop the opening of the company's Baldwin Hills store, even urging the Los Angeles Urban League not to work with Wal-Mart on a job-training program, but the head of the League turned down the unions, and more than 10,000 people applied to work in Baldwin Hills. Shoppers were just as enthusiastic about the three-level store there, a prototype for Wal-Mart in cities. In the first week the store was open, more than 330,000 customers visited the once-dying mall. "It's those who don't live in this community who did the most objecting to this store," says former Los Angeles police commissioner and now councilman Bernard Parks. "The community has clearly spoken, and it supports this store."

The experience in Baldwin Hills also refutes those who say that Wal-Mart stores drive small retailers out of business. On the contrary: barely four months after Wal-Mart opened in a once-struggling shopping center, a major real-estate outfit snapped up the center, saying that the addition of Wal-Mart gave it tremendous new potential, because other stores now wanted to move in—bringing new jobs to a depressed neighborhood. "The easiest way to fill a shopping center is to tell stores that a Wal-Mart is coming there," says Harry Freeman, executive director of the Hartford, Connecticut, Economic Development Council.

Wal-Mart's pay scales aren't the only thing that unions and their allies fear, however. A restless innovator constantly forcing other corporations to follow it, Wal-Mart is now pushing to limit soaring health-care costs by embracing a fundamental redefinition of health insurance. Wal-Mart sees it as protection from catastrophic illnesses that can financially ruin employees, rather than a benefit meant to pay for every health-care bill. In this, Wal-Mart endorses the many health-policy reformers who say that current corporate and government health plans, offering lavish coverage with little contribution from workers, have encouraged overuse of the system and helped spark runaway medical inflation. To discourage that, Wal-Mart's health plans have high deductibles and don't pay for extras such as eye exams, chiropractic visits, or contraceptives. But the company will pay 100 percent of an individual's health-care costs beyond $1,750 and has no lifetime caps on coverage—unlike more than half of other companies. As a result of its policies, Wal-Mart spends about 37 percent less per covered employee on health insurance than do similar companies.

Unions oppose Wal-Mart's approach by claiming that taxpayers foot the bill for all this, because the retailer's workers are so low paid that some opt out of Wal-Mart's health plan, despite its low cost, and use Medicaid instead. Representative Miller's congressional report on Wal-Mart estimates that each super center that opens in California would cost taxpayers $100,000 a year in federally subsidized health care, based on estimates of workers who don't sign up for Wal-Mart plans—implying, falsely, that Wal-Mart's low prices depend upon an indirect government subsidy. But at all companies, not just Wal-Mart, some young workers always decline to join the health plan, believing that they are too healthy to need it. Moreover, there is little evidence that vast numbers of Wal-Mart workers are actually not covered: as is typical of businesses with many entry-level and part-time workers, up to 40 percent of Wal-Mart's employees have health coverage under spouses' or parents' policies. Similarly, many of the retirees Wal-Mart employs as greeters have health benefits through their retirement programs.

Nonetheless, California grocery unions waged a bitter four-and-a-half-month strike over grocers' demands that employees pay a bigger share of their health-insurance premiums because of competition from Wal-Mart. Although Democratic presidential candidate John Kerry walked the picket line, the union eventually agreed to increase worker contributions to health premiums. But in this battle you can clearly see the terms of the left's coming campaign against U.S. employers' efforts to contain health-care costs.

Although union-sponsored campaigns have meant little to consumers, the constant attacks are starting to hit home with the elite media, whose members rarely go to Wal-Mart and can't understand the importance of the company's stores to middle-American shoppers. Once celebrated in the press for Sam Walton's folksy wisdom and straight-shootin' talk, Wal-Mart is just as likely to be portrayed today as an unfeeling corporate giant trying to force low prices and demanding notions of efficiency on suppliers, and imposing redneck cultural values on an unsuspecting nation.

That's evident in stories with headlines like IS WAL-MART
TOO POWERFUL? or THE WAL-MART YOU DON'T KNOW, or GOD AND
SATAN IN BENTONVILLE, which advance the party line that
Wal-Mart's business model is undermining the buying
power of the American worker and therefore has, in *Business Week*'s words, "perverse consequences" for the American economy—an unexpected judgment for a journal
claiming economic literacy. In its rush to pile on Wal-Mart,
the press seems increasingly willing to advance any disrep-
utable idea, including the demonstrably false argument
that Wal-Mart on balance costs Americans jobs by buying
goods from overseas.

Business Week, for instance, which describes the retailer
as "a cult masquerading as a company," quotes critics who
excoriate Wal-Mart for lobbying to thwart tariffs on foreign
goods, when few legitimate economists even on the left believe that high tariffs would be good for the American consumer or the U.S. economy.

Some of the critical drumbeat doubtless reflects the fact
that Wal-Mart and its founding family still promote causes
and values that the mainstream media oppose. Sam Walton
supported conservative and free-market groups. His family
has continued his tradition, supporting groups like the
Institute for Justice, a libertarian public interest law firm
that frequently represents small business against government regulation; and the National Right to Work Legal
Defense and Education Foundation, which fights compul-
sory unionism. Walton's son John is a key supporter of
charter schools and school vouchers, donating $50 million
for scholarships to send low-income students to private
schools. In 2003 the family foundation supported fifty-
seven charter schools around the country and contributed

to pro-voucher organizations like the Milton and Rose D. Friedman Foundation and the Florida Education Reform Initiative of New York City's Manhattan Institute.

The stores themselves still reflect Sam Walton's values and draw fire for it. In light of its vast market power, Wal-Mart has infuriated the media with its long-standing refusal to stock obscene CDs and racy magazines. *Business Week* branded the company a cultural gatekeeper that has "served to narrow the mainstream for entertainment offerings while imparting to it a rightward tilt." *Playboy* magazine, which Wal-Mart has refused to sell, was more blunt in its recent, lengthy anti–Wal-Mart diatribe, which called Bentonville "the epicenter of retailing's Evil Empire." So striking have the attacks been that a Kansas City business columnist recently suggested that the national press is "angry that average Americans don't share their perceptions of Wal-Mart as the bad guys" and that Wal-Mart "has come to represent the defining cultural divide between the elites and the common folk." In other words, the press doesn't like the fact that most Americans share the company's values.

Not surprisingly, the press attacks downplay Wal-Mart's many virtues: that it has never been accused of funny accounting; that it doesn't load its executives with exorbitant salaries or perks; and that, despite its market power, it doesn't charge vendors "slotting" fees—which are little more than bribes to stock their goods. By contrast with journalists, U.S. executives voted Wal-Mart America's most admired company in *Fortune* magazine's annual survey in 2003. Manufacturers, meanwhile, ranked Wal-Mart the best retailer to do business with, according to an annual survey by Cannondale Associates, while nearly three in ten shoppers surveyed by the WSL Strategic Retail consulting firm voted Wal-Mart their favorite store, a higher percentage of praise than any other retailer won.

But acclaim from the marketplace or from common folk may not protect a company when elite opinion turns against it, influencing legislators, regulators, and the courts. Wal-Mart has now become a tempting target. "We've seen many of our opponents come after us governmentally and in the media, where they see us as most vulnerable," said Jay Allen, the company's senior vice president of corporate affairs, recently. Wal-Mart made national headlines when federal agents raided independent contractors using illegal aliens to clean the company's stores. Government sources claim that Wal-Mart knew of the illegals, but the retailer says it was cooperating in a three-year government investigation and was shocked when agents ignored the deal and swooped into its stores, creating a "media frenzy," in the words of a Wal-Mart's spokesperson. Moreover Wal-Mart points out that, like other companies, it has been caught in the middle of conflicting government policies. Several years ago the INS fined the company for violating the privacy of some workers when it tried to find out if they were illegal aliens.

Encouraged by press criticism, entrepreneurial trial lawyers, eyeing Wal-Mart's deep pockets with glee, have made it perhaps the biggest private-sector target of the nation's plaintiffs' bar. In just ten years the number of pending lawsuits against Wal-Mart has increased fourfold, to eight thousand, and the company has tripled the size of its litigation department. A Tennessee trial lawyer has even created a service called the Wal-Mart Litigation Project, which, for a fee, provides information to attorneys who want to sue Wal-Mart.

Wal-Mart faces a growing number of potentially costly class-action lawsuits, exemplified by a sex-discrimination suit brought by the Cohen, Milstein, Hausfeld and Toll firm, notorious for getting Texaco to pay $176 million to black employees in a discrimination suit. That suit hinged on secretly recorded meetings in which managers reportedly made racial slurs—though subsequent audio enhancement of the tapes showed that the managers had uttered no such slurs and that the transcripts furnished by Cohen, Milstein to the *New York Times* had inaccurately represented the conversations.

So far, Cohen, Milstein has made no such "explosive" revelations in the Wal-Mart case, but to read over the lawsuit is to gain a depressing lesson in the state of employment class-action lawsuits. The suit is a collection of anecdotes of individual female employees—many of whom received poor evaluations and were turned down for promotion—who now claim that Wal-Mart managers have frustrated their career ambitions. Of the first two plaintiffs who claim that Wal-Mart passed them over for promotions because they were female, one was disciplined for admittedly returning late from lunch breaks, and the other was suspended for improper handling of a customer refund. A few other cases involve accusations of supervisors making discriminatory remarks toward female employees—entirely possible in a company with more than 1 million employees, but hardly amounting to a company-wide pattern of discrimination. Still, the lawyers claim a plaintiff's class of 700,000 current and former Wal-Mart female employees, and they argue that Wal-Mart has a long history of hostility toward women in management, starting when Sam Walton would take his executives quail hunting, which the suit avers "made women feel uncomfortable."

To rein in Wal-Mart, the left will have to maintain its assault in the courts, the statehouses, and the media, because it can't win the battle for the hearts and minds of consumers. In a recent report on shopping patterns, WSL Strategic Retail said that Wal-Mart has succeeded like no other company in understanding what consumers want and giving it to them. Despite Wal-Mart's years of success, the report predicted, the future looks even more favorable for the company and others that operate with its low-price, big-store philosophy.

To succeed against Wal-Mart, then, the left will have to fight to deny the vast majority of Americans what they want. Every battle it wins in that war will cost the American consumer plenty.

FOUR

. . . .

The Prophets of Victimology

In the 1960s a young, radical journalist helped ignite the War on Poverty with his pioneering book *The Other America*. In its pages, Michael Harrington warned that the recently proclaimed age of affluence was a mirage, that beneath the surface of U.S. prosperity lay tens of millions of people stuck in hopeless poverty that only massive government intervention could help.

Today a new generation of journalists is straining to duplicate Harrington's feat—to convince contemporary America that its economic system doesn't work for millions and that only government can lift them out of poverty. These new journalists face a tougher task than Harrington's, though, because all levels of government have spent about $10 trillion on poverty programs since his book appeared, with disappointing, even counterproductive, results. And over the last four decades, millions of poor people, immigrants and native-born alike, have risen from poverty without recourse to the government programs that Harrington inspired.

But brushing aside the War on Poverty's failure and the success of so many in climbing America's economic ladder, this generation of authors dusts off the old argument for a new era. Books like Barbara Ehrenreich's *Nickel and Dimed* and David Shipler's *The Working Poor* tell us that the poor are doing exactly what America expects of them—finding jobs, rising early to get to work every day, chasing the American dream—but that our system of "carnivorous capitalism" is so heavily arrayed against them that they can't rise out of poverty or live a decent life. These new anthems of despair paint their subjects as forced off welfare by uncompassionate conservatives and trapped in low-wage jobs that lead nowhere. They claim, too, that the good life that the country's expanding middle class enjoys rests on the backs of these working poor and their inexpensive labor, so that prosperous Americans *owe* them more tax-funded help.

Although these books resolutely ignore four decades' worth of lessons about poverty, they have found a large audience. The commentariat loves them. Leftish professors have made them required course reading. And Democratic candidates made their themes central to the 2004 elections. So it's worth looking closely at what these books contend, and at the economic realities they distort.

To begin with, they follow Harrington's 1962 classic by seeing the poor as victims of forces over which they have no control. From the hills of Appalachia to the streets of Harlem, Harrington had found a generation of impoverished former sharecroppers whose jobs had been replaced by mechanization. For them, the advances that enriched everyone else spelled disaster: "progress is misery" and "hopelessness is the message." Unprepared for life off the farm, many could never find productive work, Harrington argued, and would need perpetual government aid.

But the new thinkers quickly veer to the left of Harrington, following some of his more radical acolytes whose theories produced the War on Poverty's most spectacular disasters. Harrington had seen the poor as victims because they could find no work; his more radical allies, especially a group associated with Columbia University's social work school, argued that compelling the demoralized inner-city poor to work or take part in training that would fit them for work, instead of giving them unconditional welfare, was itself victimization. Richard A. Cloward and Frances Fox Piven, for example, argued that America's poverty programs—"self-righteously oriented toward getting people off welfare" and making them independent—were violating the civil rights of the poor. The journalist Richard Elman claimed that "vindictive" America was "humiliating" welfare recipients by forcing them to seek entry-level work as taxi drivers, restaurant employees, and factory laborers instead of giving them a guaranteed minimum income.

Sympathetic mayors and welfare officials responded to Cloward and Piven's call, boosting benefits, loosening eligibility rules, and cutting investigations of welfare cheating. Welfare rolls soared, along with welfare fraud and illegitimate births. The result was a national backlash that sparked the Reagan administration's welfare spending cuts.

But the Columbia crew left its enduring mark on welfare policy, in the principle that welfare, once a short-term program to help people get back on their feet, should be continuous and come with few restrictions and no stigma. A welfare mother, screaming at New York mayor John Lindsay (responsible for much of the city's rise in welfare cases), expressed the system's new philosophy: "It's my job to have kids, Mr. Mayor, and your job to take care of them." It was a philosophy that bred an urban underclass of nonworking single mothers and fatherless children, condemned to intergenerational poverty, despite the trillions spent to help them.

Like Communists who claim that communism didn't fail but instead was never really tried, Barbara Ehrenreich made her public debut with an attempt to brush aside the War on Poverty's obviously catastrophic results. The forty-six-year-old daughter of a Montana copper miner–turned–business executive, she joined Cloward and Piven to co-author a 1987 polemic, *The Mean Season: The Attack on the Welfare State*. The War on Poverty had failed so far, the book claimed, not because of its flawed premises but because the government hadn't done enough to redistribute the nation's wealth. America needed an even bigger War on Poverty that would turn the country into a European-style social welfare state. Pooh-poohing the work ethic and the dignity of labor, the authors derided calls for welfare reform that would require recipients to work, because that would be mortifying to the poor. "There is nothing ennobling about being forced to please an employer to feed one's children," the authors wrote, forgetting that virtually every worker and business owner must please someone, whether boss or customer, to earn a living. Welfare's true purpose, the book declared, should be to "permit certain groups to opt out of work." (The authors never explained why all of us shouldn't demand the right to "opt out.")

The Mean Season's argument gained little traction, but as the nineties dawned, Ehrenreich found a way to bring

Cloward and Piven's socialistic themes successfully into the new decade and beyond. Her 1989 book, *Fear of Falling: The Inner Life of the Middle Class*, blamed poverty's continued existence in America partly on the Me Generation, which Tom Wolfe had so brilliantly made interesting to the nation. America's emerging professional middle class had started out hopefully in the 1960s, Ehrenreich claims, the inheritor of a liberating cultural revolution. But because that class depended on intellectual capital to make its living, rather than on income from property or investments, it felt a sharp economic insecurity, which by the late 1980s had made it "meaner, more selfish," and (worse still) "more hostile to the aspirations of the less fortunate," especially in its impatience with welfare.

The book vibrates with Ehrenreich's rage toward middle-class Americans. The middle class, she sneers, obsessively pursues wealth and is abjectly "sycophantic toward those who have it, impatient with those who do not." To Ehrenreich, "The nervous, uphill climb of the professional class accelerates the downward spiral of society as a whole: toward cruelly widening inequalities, toward heightened estrangement along class lines, and toward the moral anesthesia that estrangement requires." Ironically, Ehrenreich's economic prescription for a better America was for government to create one gigantic bourgeoisie: "Tax the rich and enrich the poor until both groups are absorbed into some broad and truly universal middle class. The details are subject to debate." *Time* magazine, the voice of the bourgeoisie, made her a regular columnist.

If the Reagan era could provoke Ehrenreich to such anger, it's no surprise that the 1996 welfare reform heightened her fury. Passed by a Republican-controlled Congress and signed into law by Democratic president Bill Clinton, the legislation ended welfare as an automatic federal entitlement and required states to oblige able-bodied recipients to work. The law put a five-year limit on welfare (the average stay on the rolls had been thirteen years) but exempted 20 percent of the cases—roughly equivalent to the portion of the welfare population believed too dysfunctional ever to get off public assistance. After President Clinton signed the bill, Ehrenreich claimed that she had seen the betrayal coming: she'd presciently cast a write-in vote for Ralph Nader in the 1992 presidential election. She castigated the left for its muted response to the new welfare law, though she later praised National Organization for Women president Patricia Ireland's hunger strike protesting the bill.

Ehrenreich's anger propelled her to write *Nickel and Dimed*. Beginning life as a piece of "undercover journalism" for *Harper's*, the 2001 book purports to reveal the truth about poverty in post–welfare reform America. "In particular," Ehrenreich asks in the introduction, how were "the roughly four million women about to be booted into the labor market by welfare reform . . . going to make it on $6 or $7 an hour?"

Nickel and Dimed doesn't fuss much with public-policy agendas, messy economic theories, or basic job numbers. Instead it gives us Ehrenreich's first-person account of three brief sojourns into the world of the lowest of low-wage work: as a waitress for a low-priced family restaurant in Florida; as a maid for a housecleaning service in Maine; and as a women's apparel clerk at a Minneapolis Wal-Mart. In her journeys she meets a lively and sympathetic assortment of co-workers: Haitian busboys, a Czech dishwasher, a cook with a gambling problem, and assorted single working mothers. But the focus is mostly on Ehren-reich, not her colleagues.

The point that *Nickel and Dimed* wants to prove is that in today's economy, a woman coming off welfare into a low-wage job can't earn enough to pay for basic living expenses. Rent is a burden, Ehrenreich discovers. In Florida she lands a $500-a-month efficiency apartment; in Maine she spends $120 a week for a shared apartment in an old motel (she turns down a less expensive room elsewhere because it's on a noisy commercial street); in Minneapolis she pays $255 a week for a moldy hotel room. These seem like reasonable enough rents, except perhaps for Minneapolis, judging from her description of the place. But with her entry-level wages—roughly the minimum wage (when tips are included) as a waitress, about $6 an hour as a maid, and $7 an hour to start at Wal-Mart—Ehrenreich quickly finds that she'll need a second job to support herself. This seems to startle her, as if holding down two jobs is something new to America. "In the new version of supply and demand," she writes, "jobs are so cheap—as measured by the pay—that a worker is encouraged to take on as many as she possibly can."

What's utterly misleading about Ehrenreich's exposé, though, is how she fixes the parameters of her experiment so that she inevitably gets the outcome that she wants—"proof" that the working poor can't make it. Ehrenreich complains that America's supposedly tight labor market doesn't produce entry-level jobs at ten dollars an hour. For people with no skills, that's probably true in most parts of the country; but everywhere the U.S. economy provides ample opportunity to move up quickly. Yet Ehrenreich spends only a few weeks with each of her employers, and so never gives herself the chance for promotion or to find better work (or better places to live).

In fact, few working in low-wage jobs stay in them long. And most workers don't just move on quickly—they also move on to better jobs. The Sphere Institute, a California public-policy think tank founded by Stanford University professors, charted the economic path of workers in the state from 1988 to 2000 and found extraordinary mobility across industries and up the economic ladder. Over 40 percent of the lowest income group worked in retail in 1988; by 2000 more than half of that group had switched to other industries. Their average inflation-adjusted income gain after moving on: 83 percent, to over $32,000 a year.

The workers who stayed in retail, moreover, were usually the higher earners, making about $10,000 more a year than the leavers. They had already started improving their lots back in 1988, in other words, and probably elected to stay because they rightly saw further opportunity in retailing, though the study doesn't say what happened to them. The same dynamic occurs in other industries where low-wage jobs are concentrated, the study found: those who do well stay and watch earnings go up; those who feel stuck often depart and see earnings rise too, as they find more promising jobs. In total, over twelve years, 88 percent of those in California's lowest economic category moved up, their incomes rising as they gained experience on the job and time in the workforce, two things that the marketplace rewards.

Such results are only the latest to confirm the enormous mobility that the U.S. economy offers. As a review of academic, peer-reviewed mobility studies by two Urban Institute researchers put it: "It is clear that there is substantial mobility—both short-term and long-term—over an average life-cycle in the United States." Perhaps most astonishingly, mobility often occurs within months. The Urban Institute report points out that several mobility studies based on the University of Michigan's Panel Study of Income Dynamics, which has traced thousands of American families since 1968, show that about 20 percent of those in the lowest economic quintile rise at least one economic class within a year. If Ehrenreich had given herself twelve months in her low-wage stints, instead of a week or two, she might have worked her way into the lower middle class by the end of her experiment.

This mobility explains why poverty rates didn't soar in the 1990s, even though some thirteen million people, most of them dirt-poor, immigrated here legally. In fact the country's poverty rate actually fell slightly during the nineties— which could only happen because millions already here rose out of the lowest income category.

Confidence in the American economy's capacity to foster income mobility helped impel the 1996 welfare reform in the first place. Most former welfare recipients entering the workforce, reformers believed, would over time improve their lives—at least if other handicaps such as drug or alcohol addiction and serious mental deficiencies didn't hold them back. Everything we've subsequently learned about welfare reform shows that the reformers were right, rendering Ehrenreich's book oddly dated from the outset.

Since welfare reform passed, employment among single mothers who'd never previously worked has risen 40 percent. More important, child poverty in single-mother households fell to its lowest point ever just three years after welfare reform became law. Except for a hiccup at the end of the last recession, the poverty rate among those households has continued to drop, down now by about one-third. The *New York Times* recently reported that "lawmakers of both parties describe the 1996 law as a success that moved millions of people from welfare to work and cut the welfare rolls by 60 percent, to 4.9 million people." Those results belie the hysterical warnings of welfare advocates, Ehrenreich among them, that reform would drastically worsen poverty.

Given that such data subvert Ehrenreich's case against the U.S. economic system, she unsurprisingly puts statistics aside in *Nickel and Dimed* and instead seeks to paint the low-wage workplace as oppressive and humiliating to workers forced by reformers to enter it. But given the author's self-absorption, what the reader really gets is a self-portrait of Ehrenreich as a longtime rebel with an anti-authoritarian streak a mile wide, who can't stomach the basic boundaries that most people easily accept in the workplace.

At Wal-Mart, for instance, she's "oppressed by the mandatory gentility" that the company requires of her, as if being nice to customers and co-workers were part of the tyranny of capitalism. (I suspect that most customers, if they encountered a snarling Ehrenreich as a clerk while shopping, would flee for the exit.) Told to scrub floors on her hands and knees by the maid service, she cites a "housecleaning expert" who says this technique is ineffective. Ehrenreich then theorizes that the real reason the service wants its employees down on their hands and knees is that "this primal posture of submission" and "anal accessibility" seem to "gratify the consumers of maid services." Never has the simple task of washing a floor been so thoroughly Freudianized.

In Ehrenreich's looking-glass world, opportunity becomes oppression. Hired by Wal-Mart shortly after applying, she weirdly protests that "there is no intermediate point [between applying and beginning orientation] . . . in which you confront the employer as a free agent, entitled to cut her own deal." Although she admits that in such a tight labor market "I would probably have been welcome to apply at any commercial establishment I entered," she still feels "like a supplicant with her hand stretched out."

Unable to understand why her fellow workers don't share her outrage, this longtime socialist and radical feminist turns on the very people with whom she's trying to sympathize, imagining that they can only accept their terrible exploitation because they've become psychologically incapable of resisting. Why are the maids so loyal to the owner of the cleaning service? she asks. They're so emotionally "needy" that they can't break free, she speculates. Why do Wal-Mart workers accept their place in "Mr. Sam's family" instead of rising in a tide of unionization against the company? The Waltons have hoodwinked them, she surmises, misunderstanding completely the appeal to employees of Wal-Mart's opportunity culture, where two-thirds of management has come up from hourly-employee store ranks and where workers own a good chunk of company stock.

Responsibility for America's shameful economic injustice rests not only with exploitative businesses like Wal-Mart, in Ehrenreich's view, but also with the rich and—you guessed it—the middle class. Going beyond even *Fear of Falling, Nickel and Dimed* hangs a huge guilt trip on the middle class. Actually, guilt "doesn't go anywhere near far enough," Ehrenreich says. "[T]he appropriate emotion," she claims, "is shame—shame at our own dependency, in this case, on the underpaid labor of others." After all, Ehrenreich tells us, it's the middle class and its irritation with the poor that led to the catastrophe of welfare reform. "When poor single mothers had the option of remaining out of the labor force on welfare, the middle and upper middle class tended to view them with a certain impatience, if not disgust," she maintains.

Like some of Ehrenreich's earlier work, *Nickel and Dimed* is contemptuous of ordinary Americans. Cleaning the homes of middle-class families, she snoops in bookcases and finds mostly writers on the "low end of the literary spectrum"— you know, Grisham, Limbaugh, those kinds of authors. "Mostly though, books are for show," she clairvoyantly concludes. A woman whose home furnishings suggest that she is a Martha Stewart "acolyte" comes in for particularly withering scorn. "Everything about [her home] enrages me," Ehrenreich snaps. She's only slightly less condescending toward the lower middle class. She mocks Wal-Mart's customers for being obese—or at least the "native Caucasians" among them. Ehrenreich doesn't say what she thinks about the body types of middle-income blacks, Latinos, or Asians.

Ehrenreich's disparagement of the middle class, Wal-Mart, Martha Stewart, and various other targets of the left these days doubtless has a lot to do with *Nickel and Dimed*'s remarkable success. The book rode the *New York Times* hardcover best-seller list for eighteen weeks and has been on the paperback best-seller list for nearly two years now. So far it has sold upward of a half-million copies in the United States.

The left-leaning professoriat is helping drive the sales. *Nickel and Dimed* is standard fare in many freshman-orientation reading programs, in which schools require an

entire incoming class to read one particular book. Among
the twenty or so schools that have selected *Nickel and
Dimed* for such programs are Ohio State (fourteen thousand freshmen), the University of California, Riverside
(nearly twenty thousand freshmen), and Ball State (eight
thousand-plus freshmen). Some of the schools, including
Mansfield University in Pennsylvania (freshman class
about sixteen hundred), have bought the book for students just to ensure that the kids don't miss out on its wisdom. Since the book's publication, Ehrenreich enthuses,
she's lectured at more than a hundred universities.

Not everyone is taking this force-feeding of leftist propaganda sitting down. Conservative students at the University of North Carolina at Chapel Hill protested the
freshman-orientation reading committee's choice of *Nickel
and Dimed*, bringing in local conservative groups and state
legislators to try to force greater ideological balance on the
school's reading program. What students objected to, explains Michael McKnight, a UNC grad who helped lead the
protest, was the book's biased and misleading depiction of
the American workplace, along with UNC's failure to provide any counterweight, such as critical reviews of the
book. Says McKnight, "The freshman-orientation package
of resources on the book included nothing but glowing reviews of it and lists of Ehrenreich's awards."

There's other evidence that students aren't buying Ehrenreich's pessimistic line on the U.S. economy. Professor Larry
Schweikart, who teaches U.S. economic history at the University of Dayton, assigns his students *Nickel and Dimed*
along with other books that paint a brighter picture of the
American economy. Schweikart says that many students
quickly grasp what's wrong with Ehrenreich's book. "Many

of these kids have worked in the low-wage marketplace, so they are more familiar with it than their professors or media reviewers. They tell me that there are better jobs out there than the ones Ehrenreich stuck herself with, that those jobs aren't long-term, and that they understand that she didn't give herself any time to find better work or advance."

If the holes in Ehrenreich's argument are clear even to some college kids, the logical gaps gape even wider in the 2004 book that hopes to succeed *Nickel and Dimed* as the definitive left statement on the oppressiveness of low-wage work: *The Working Poor,* by former *New York Times* reporter David Shipler. To his credit, Shipler, unlike Ehrenreich, cares enough about the workers who are his subjects to try to give a comprehensive account of their struggles to make it, delving into their lives and addressing important economic and cultural issues head-on. Following Ehrenreich, however, Shipler wants to blame an unjust U.S. economy for the plight of the poor. Yet his own evidence proves a very different, and crucial, point: it's often dysfunctional behavior and bad choices, not a broken economy, that prevent people from escaping poverty.

Consider some of the former welfare recipients Shipler profiles in his chapter called "Work Doesn't Work." Christie, a day-care worker, describes herself as "lazy" for never finishing college (her brother, who did, is an accountant, and her sister is a loan officer). She has had several children out of wedlock with various men, and now lives with one of them—Kevin, an ex-con—in public housing. Christie can't make ends meet, but that's partly because, having never learned to cook, she blows her $138-a-month food-stamp allocation on "an abundance of high-priced, well-advertised snacks, junk food, and prepared meals."

Then there's Debra, who had her first illegitimate child at eighteen. Forced to work by welfare reform, Debra actually lands a job in a unionized factory—the holy grail of low-wage work to the left. Unfortunately she can't adjust to work in the shop, has nightmares about the assembly line, and imagines that the bosses prefer the Hispanic workers to her, since she's black. Shipler understands that with such attitudes, she is unlikely to move up.

Or how about Caroline, who spent years on welfare and has worked various jobs, including at Wal-Mart? She actually owns her own house, though, as Shipler ominously mentions, "it is mostly owned by the bank." (Welcome to the club, Caroline.) Caroline is a victim of the "ruthlessness of the market system," Shipler informs us, because she can't seem to land a promotion. We eventually learn from her caseworkers, however, that she doesn't bathe regularly and smells bad, that when she first divorced she refused her in-laws' offer of help, that she then married a man who beat her (she later left him), and that she keeps managing to get hired but then loses one job after another.

How has the U.S. economy let these workers down? In each of these cases, bad choices have kept someone from getting ahead.

Shipler's grim chapter headings are often wildly at odds with the stories he tells. One chapter, "Harvest of Shame," describes Hispanic seasonal farmworkers who toil long hours for little money, often live in substandard temporary quarters, yearn for their families, and—because many are here illegally—don't qualify for government benefits. Again, though, is the U.S. economic system really exploiting these workers, as Shipler thinks? We soon learn that many of the illegals have come here to support families back in Mexico.

They send home 70 percent of what they earn and plan to return south when they've amassed enough wealth (by Mexican standards).

True, since they're illegals they can't get mainstream jobs with the potential for promotion and benefits. Yet for them this low-wage work pays off. Pedro earns nine times more working illegally on a North Carolina farm than he did toiling in a Mexican slaughterhouse. He sends from $300 to $500 a month home to his folks. If he works just two more years on the farm, he figures, he'll have enough to build a house in Mexico, and it'll be time to go home. Like many of his countrymen, Pedro is temporarily using America to make up for the Mexican economy's deficiencies. This hardly represents a failure of our economy. Shipler nonetheless finds puzzling the "absence of anger" among these immigrants.

Pointing to illegals like Pedro, who can't take advantage of the larger opportunities that our economy offers, or to people like Debra and Christie, who, every time they start to climb the economic ladder, do something self-destructive that causes them to fall back a few rungs, Shipler claims that economic mobility is vanishing from the United States. Today, he says, low-wage workers can only better themselves if they benefit from a "perfect lineup of favorable conditions."

The Tran family is just such an exception, Shipler thinks. Everything works for these Vietnamese immigrants. Within four months of arriving in the United States in 1998, three family members were working, earning $42,848 in their first year in the country. Within five months the family had earned enough to buy two used cars. Within two years, two children had registered for college. This is a "heroic" success story, in Shipler's view, because for low-wage workers in today's America, "there is no room for mistake or misfortune—not for drugs, not for alcohol, not for domestic violence."

But what the Trans have done, admirable as it is, isn't heroic—or even unusual. In 1990s California, where the Trans did so well, recall that nearly nine of ten low-wage workers moved up, presumably avoiding the drugs, alcohol, and violence that Shipler wrongly sees as endemic to poverty. The average real income of the low-wage workers in the Sphere Institute study doubled over that time to more than $27,000 a year. Nor is there any evidence, statistically or anecdotally, that such mobility is disappearing from the United States.

For Shipler, as for Ehrenreich, the United States always shortchanges the poor. Education is a prime example, he says. He tours Washington, D.C.'s public schools, where student scores are abysmal and dropout rates are inexcusably high, and—noticing the classrooms' shortages of supplies and books and the nonexistent computers—says that lack of money is to blame. But the notorious failure of D.C.'s public schools has nothing to do with money. Those schools spend some $13,500 per pupil a year—not as much as rich suburban districts, true, but far above the national average and well above what many private schools spend to educate kids effectively. As for the missing supplies and computers, blame a corrupt, dysfunctional system that wastes the more than adequate funds. There's no hint of this ongoing scandal in Shipler's book, even though for years the local papers have chronicled it extensively and, in desperation, Mayor Williams and the U.S. Congress have set up a voucher plan to address it.

Shipler's obliviousness to the real causes of poverty also characterizes the latest addition to the "working poor" canon: Joanna Lipper's *Growing Up Fast*. A sometime documentary filmmaker, Lipper traveled to the once-thriving industrial town of Pittsfield, Massachusetts, in order to chronicle the lives of a generation of teenage unwed mothers. Because many of these young women are daughters of blue-collar workers who lost their jobs as General Electric gradually pulled out of Pittsfield during the 1980s, Lipper blames G.E. and, more broadly, globalization for the social pathology evident in the town today—not just the teen pregnancies but also the rising crime and drug-abuse rates that she says followed G.E.'s departure. The town's youth "have been excluded from the American dream," she writes.

Yet as the tale of Pittsfield and its teens unfolds, a different story emerges, even if Lipper—like Shipler in this regard—seems not to grasp the meaning of her own evidence. We learn, for example, that the town's drug problem actually began in the early 1980s, before G.E. left, after social-services providers opened government-funded drug-treatment centers in the area and imported hundreds of addicts from New York City and elsewhere to receive treatment. Many of these addicts, released from the programs but not fully detoxed, stayed on. They then brought friends and relatives to town and started dealing drugs around local fast-food joints and other spots where teens hung out. Not that all the buyers were kids, let alone "excluded" ones. Fueling the market, we learn, were "doctors from Williamstown and well-to-do people."

The teens get pregnant, as Lipper tells it, because they've got nothing better to do. They feel trapped because "the major institutions of American life," the job market heading

87

the list, "are not working for them," Lipper says. "[H]ope is the ingredient missing" from their lives. Yet one teen mother, Jessica, confides: "I had so much going for me before I got pregnant." Another, Shayla, herself born to teen parents long before job woes came to Pittsfield, says that she wanted to attend college but didn't work hard enough in high school to get in.

It never occurs to Lipper that teen pregnancy doesn't naturally flow from economic status. After all, millions of impoverished immigrants came to America from Europe in the early twentieth century without illegitimacy getting out of hand, thanks to strong religious traditions that stigmatized illegitimacy. What's really missing from the lives of Pittsfield's unwed mothers isn't hope; it's shame about teenage sex or out-of-wedlock pregnancy. The teens talk openly of early sexual escapades and matter-of-factly pose for book photos with their illegitimate kids—unsurprising in a culture that glorifies sex and in which movie stars and rock musicians proudly flaunt their out-of-wedlock offspring. The demise of shame is a far more plausible explanation for Pittsfield's teen-pregnancy problem than is economic distress.

Like Shipler, in other words, Lipper has reversed cause and effect. She sees social dysfunction in Pittsfield and blames it on poverty. But it typically is personal failure and social dysfunction that create poverty. To stay out of poverty in America, it's necessary to do three simple things, social scientists have found: finish high school, don't have kids until you marry, and wait until you are at least twenty to marry. Do those three things and the odds against your becoming impoverished are less than one in ten. Nearly 80 percent of everyone who fails to do those three things winds up poor.

That's a crucial truth that left-wing social thinkers have tried to deny from the earliest days of the welfare-rights movement. And as these books show, even after the conclusive failure of the War on Poverty and the resounding success of welfare reform, they are still at it.

. . . .

The Curse of the Creative Class

Providence, Rhode Island, is so worried that it doesn't appeal to hip, young technology workers that local economic-development officials are urging a campaign to make the city the nation's capital of independent rock music. In Pittsburgh, another place that fears it lacks appeal among talented young people, officials want to build bike paths and outdoor hiking trails to make the city a magnet for creative workers. Meanwhile a Memphis economic-development group is pressing that city to hold "celebrations of diversity" to attract more gays and minorities, in order—in their view—to bolster the local economy.

If you think these efforts represent some fringe of economic development, think again. All of these cities have been inspired by the theories of Richard Florida, a George Mason University professor whose notion that cities must become trendy, happening places in order to compete in the twenty-first-century economy is sweeping urban America. In his popular book *The Rise of the Creative Class*, Florida argues that cities that attract gays, bohemians, and ethnic minorities are the new economic powerhouses because they are also the places where creative workers—the kind who start and staff innovative, fast-growing companies—want to live. To lure this workforce, Florida argues, cities must dispense with stuffy old theories of economic development—like the notion that low taxes are what draw in companies and workers—and instead must spend heavily on cultural amenities and pursue progressive social legislation.

A generation of leftish policymakers and urban planners is rushing to implement Florida's vision while an admiring host of uncritical journalists touts it. But there is just one problem: the basic economics behind his ideas don't work. Far from being economic powerhouses, a number of the cities that the professor identifies as creative-age winners have chronically underperformed the American economy. And, though Florida is fond of saying that today "place matters" in attracting workers and business, some of his top creative cities don't even do a particularly good job at attracting—or keeping—residents. Before the rest of urban America embraces the professor's trendy nostrums, let's take a closer look at them in practice.

Richard Florida's work first began attracting attention because he sought to explain what new-economy workers and their companies valued to a generation of urban politicians and policy wonks baffled by the late-1990s tech boom. Many municipal officials during those heady years suddenly found their cities populated with youthful entrepreneurs whose new companies had struck it rich in the stock market or with venture capitalists. These Internet kids, largely playing with other people's money, sought to move their hot businesses into cool neighborhoods with architecturally rich traditions, where they installed basketball courts in their new offices, held meetings with their dogs prancing about, and hired young, single workers like themselves, who worried more about a city's music scene than its personal income-tax rates.

Florida, who started his career as an academic economist writing dry treatises on industrial production, began contemplating this world when Carnegie Mellon enlisted him to help Pittsburgh attract and retain more educated workers and high-tech firms. He observed in the mid-1990s that cities reputed to be cool, "in" places seemed to be incubating many of the hottest new technology companies, and he began to wonder if, in the jargon of academia, some new paradigm was emerging, based on the "lifestyle choices" of a new generation of workers. In 1998 he met a Carnegie Mellon graduate student, Gary Gates, who was tracking U.S. gay communities using Census Bureau statistics on unmarried same-sex households. In what he describes as a major revelation, Florida noticed that Gates's list of America's most gay-friendly cities closely matched his list of hip technology centers. Looking for other ways to measure the distinguishing characteristics of the new-economy cities, Florida developed a so-called Bohemian Index, which counted the number of artists, writers, and performers in a city. He added a Creative Class Index to measure a city's concentration of knowledge workers—scientists, engineers, professors, think-tank employees. Each index, Florida was stunned to find, correlated highly with the other indexes. Cities with many gays were also places with lots of performers, creative workers, and tech companies.

At this point Florida made two big—and dubious—leaps of logic. First, he assumed there was a causal connection linking all these indexes to economic growth. Then he decided that he could infer just what it was about these cities that helped power this growth. He concluded that in the new economic order, the engine of growth wasn't individual companies but, rather, creative workers, who came to live in cities they admired and then started their own firms or attracted businesses seeking educated workers. What enticed these workers, the professor concluded with very little evidence, was that the cities were "tolerant, diverse and open to creativity."

Florida found a ready audience for his ideas on the lecture circuit, then refined and expanded them in *The Rise of the Creative Class*, which reads more like a pop cultural and social history of the Internet generation than an economic-development treatise. Sprinkled with references to Baudelaire, Bob Dylan, T. S. Eliot, and Isaac Newton, *The Rise of the Creative Class* is largely a recounting of the 1990s technology explosion, with chapters devoted to such already familiar subjects as the casual dress revolution ("The No-Collar Workplace") and the tendency of young tech workers to toil long hours ("The Time Warp"). Eager to demonstrate that he is as hip as the people he writes about, Florida describes talented young software engineers as rock stars, labels one of his chapters "a rant," and approvingly describes a business conference where attendees were issued Wiffle balls to pelt speakers with whom they disagreed.

While much of *The Rise of the Creative Class* is little more than Florida's depiction of the Internet bubble's go-go culture, the last third of the book offers urban policymakers a seemingly dazzling new economic-development agenda derived from these observations. To capitalize on the hot new economy, Florida tells policymakers, they must reach out to the creative class, whose interests are different from those of the buttoned-down families that cities traditionally try to attract through good schools and low taxes. The new creative class craves a vibrant nightlife, outdoor sports facilities, and neighborhoods vibrant with street performers, unique shops, and chic cafés. In Florida's universe, the number of local bands on the pop charts becomes more important to the economy than tax codes. "It is hard to think of a major high-tech region that doesn't have a distinct audio identity," Florida writes, sounding more like a rock critic than an economics prof. Creative workers want to live and work in "authentic" neighborhoods of historic buildings, not areas that are "full of chain stores, chain restaurants and nightclubs," he asserts. Accordingly, cities should stop approving expansive new condo developments on their outer boundaries and instead focus on retooling former warehouse and factory districts.

It isn't all rock music, antique architecture, and snowboarding, however. Workers also seek enlightened communities and employers who encourage differences. In focus groups, Florida says, young knowledge workers say they are drawn to places "known for diversity of thought and open-mindedness." For example, young heterosexual workers tell Florida that they seek out companies that offer domestic-partner benefits, not because they plan to use them but because such benefits signal that the company practices the kind of tolerance they approve of.

According to Florida, the winners in an age that values these attributes include gay-friendly San Francisco, laid-back Austin, multicultural New York, and progressive Minneapolis. Florida advises leaders of cities trying to emulate this group to ensure that their towns remain "open to diversity" by promoting laws that creative types see as welcoming, while guarding against social legislation that makes their cities seem less tolerant. (Although the professor isn't explicit in his book about what kinds of laws attract the creative class, he told a Canadian newspaper that "the legalization of gay marriage is one of the great talent attraction packages of the last hundred years.") Political leaders should also invest in "lifestyle amenities," such as bike paths (an obsession of Florida's) and running and Rollerblading trails. Cities should follow the example of Austin, where public television features live music festivals and where city leaders require companies that want to expand downtown to contribute to an arts and culture fund.

Following this prescription, Florida tells us, there's hope for any city, even his decidedly unhip former hometown. Under the professor's spell, Pittsburgh is working on becoming a creative talent magnet. One sure sign that its prospects are brightening, Florida tells us: the Showtime cable network chose the city as the location for the series *Queer as Folk*. Can prosperity be far behind?

It's not hard to see why Florida's ideas would have wide appeal. His book has struck a chord among a generation of young, tech-oriented workers and entrepreneurs—the *Fast Company* magazine crowd that Florida is writing about—because rather than bash their go-go, Silicon Valley culture, as critics from both the left and the right have done for different reasons, Florida celebrates it. *The Rise of the Creative Class* also appeals to a broader group of young, educated workers, who, as David Brooks describes in *Bobos in Paradise*, have managed to combine two traditions that had

95

previously been at odds—the bourgeois work ethic with bohemian culture—into something new, which Florida calls
his "creative class." To such people, work offers spiritual as
well as economic gratification. They may come to the office
dressed in jeans and sneakers, but they happily work
twelve-hour days, view their co-workers as close friends,
and look to their jobs for a sense of personal fulfillment,
growth, and even identity. Unlike Brooks, who gently sati-
rizes these bobos, Florida regards them as a powerful and
admirable new capitalist class that state and local policymakers should court enthusiastically.

Florida's ideas also spark enthusiasm among the advocates of public funding of cultural institutions and the arts.
Florida gives them a rationale for ever more government
support. Iowa's director of cultural affairs, Anita Walker,
spouts pure Floridese when she declares, "Culture is no
longer a frill. It is [economic] fuel."

But most important to a generation of liberal urban policymakers and politicians who favor big government,
Florida's ideas offer a way to talk economic-development
talk while walking the familiar big-spending walk. In the
old rhetorical paradigm, left-wing politicians often paid little heed to what mainstream businesses—those that create
the bulk of jobs—wanted or needed, except when individual
firms threatened to leave town, at which point municipal
officials might grudgingly offer tax incentives. The business
community was otherwise a giant cash register to be tapped
for public revenues—an approach that sparked a steady
drain of businesses and jobs out of the big cities once technology freed them from the necessity of staying there.

Now comes Florida with the equivalent of an eat-all-
you-want-and-still-lose-weight diet. Yes, you can create

needed revenue-generating jobs without having to take the unpalatable measures—shrinking government and cutting taxes—that appeal to old-economy businessmen, the kind with starched shirts and lodge pins in their lapels. You can bypass all that and go straight to the new economy, where the future is happening now. You can draw in Florida's creative-class capitalists—ponytails, jeans, rock music, and all—by liberal, big-government means: diversity celebrations, "progressive" social legislation, and government spending on cultural amenities. Put another way, Florida's ideas are breathing new life into an old argument: that taxes, incentives, and business-friendly policies are less important in attracting jobs than social legislation and government-provided amenities. After all, if New York can flourish with its high tax rates and Austin can boom with its heavy regulatory environment and limits on development, any city can thrive in the new economy.

Armed with such notions, cities across North America, Europe, and as far afield as New Zealand are rushing to implement the professor's ideas. Cincinnati, its image battered by race riots in 2001, is in the process of being Floridazed: it invested $1.3 million in the requisite bike path and in a recreation area stretching from downtown to the airport, and it has put another $2.2 million into a cultural fund, which it plans to invest in "edgy" arts groups in an effort to create a bohemian "street culture." Among its grants: $40,000 to a local blues music society. Supporters of a Florida-inspired group, Cincinnati Tomorrow, are also lobbying to overturn legislation, spearheaded by local black churches, that opponents say makes the city less gay-friendly.

Despite a budget deficit, the State of Iowa has put aside tens of millions of dollars for a cultural/economic plan, including $45 million for "community attractions" ranging from hiking trails to entertainment districts in the state. Advocates of Richard Florida's ideas in Iowa managed to win the money even though, as a sympathetic state legislator recounts, "We have a hard time convincing rural legislators that arts and culture are key to future economic growth." One can just imagine that conversation.

Austin, already one of the winners in Florida's world, is working hard to keep its edge. The city sets aside taxes on hotel rooms and car rentals to support local artists. A city council economic-development subcommittee has adopted the slogan "Keep Austin Weird" to emphasize its belief that support for offbeat culture is essential to the city's economic future. One defining assertion of that conviction, as Florida approvingly reports, is that Austin has erected—right smack in the midst of its downtown jogging trail—a bronze statue honoring not Sam Houston or Jim Bowie but rock guitarist Stevie Ray Vaughan.

Florida's ideas are making headway in Canada too. Former Winnipeg mayor Glen Murray nearly doubled arts spending, despite the city's tight budget and complaints from businesses and residents about high taxes and inadequate basic services. Responding to critics of proposed tax increases to pay for his nostrums, Murray said in pure Floridese: "What kills a city are people who want only low taxes, only want a good deal and only want cities to be about . . . pipes, pavement and policing."

But cities rushing to embrace Florida's ideas have based their strategies more on wishful thinking than clear-eyed analysis. Neither the professor nor his most ardent adherents seem worried that the Internet generation formed its eccentric capitalist culture during a speculative bubble, when billions of dollars of free-flowing investment capital gave workers and their bosses the freedom to ignore basic economic concerns, and that now, with that money vanished and many companies defunct, a focus on such old-economy ideas as profits and tax rates has reemerged.

Moreover, as Florida's ideas reach beyond urban-planning types and New Age liberal politicians, they are at some point likely to find resistance from the hard-core urban left, composed increasingly of social-services activists and representatives of public-employee and service-industry unions, who demand ever more government spending for social programs, not arts and culture. Indeed, the professor's relentless argument that governments should help furnish bobo-friendly amenities ultimately comes to sound like a new form of class warfare: old-economy workers have no place in his utopian dreams.

But a far more serious—indeed, fatal—objection to Florida's theories is that the economics behind them don't work. Although Florida's book bristles with charts and statistics showing how he constructed his various indexes and where cities rank on them, the professor, incredibly, doesn't provide any data demonstrating that his creative cities actually have vibrant economies that perform well over time. A look at even the most simple economic indicators, in fact, shows that, far from being economic powerhouses, many of Florida's favored cities are chronic underperformers.

Exhibit A is the most fundamental economic measure, job growth. The professor's Creativity Index—a composite of his other indexes—lists San Francisco, Austin, Houston, and San Diego among the top ten. His bottom ten include New Orleans, Las Vegas, Memphis, and Oklahoma City, which he says are "stuck in paradigms of old economic development" and are losing their "economic dynamism" to his winners. So you'd expect his winners to be big job producers. Yet for ten years starting at the beginning of the tech boom in 1993, cities that score the best on Florida's analysis actually grew no faster than the overall U.S. jobs economy, increasing their employment base by only slightly more than 17 percent. Florida's indexes, in fact, are such poor predictors of economic performance that his top cities didn't even outperform his bottom ones. Led by big percentage gains in Las Vegas (the fastest-growing local economy in the nation) as well as in Oklahoma City and Memphis, Florida's ten least creative cities turn out to be jobs powerhouses, adding more than 19 percent to their job totals for a decade—faster growth even than the national economy.

Florida's ten most creative midsize cities are even less impressive economic engines. During the same ten-year span these cities, which include such underperformers as Albany, New York, and Dayton, Ohio, increased their job totals by about 16 percent—less than the national average.

But Florida rarely lets basic economic data get in the way of his theories. Since the Internet meltdown, for instance, he has said that, though some of his most creative cities don't seem to be doing very well these days, their performance shouldn't be viewed so narrowly. "These places have been growing for decades, building solid new industries that have helped to strengthen our economy," he writes. But this simply isn't true. Jobs data going back twenty years, to 1983, show that Florida's top ten cities as a group actually do worse, lagging behind the national economy by several percentage points, while his so-called least creative cities continue to look like jobs powerhouses, expanding 60 percent faster than his most creative cities during that same period. None of this is surprising: given that many of Florida's most creative cities are so tech-oriented, the further back one looks, to the days before the tech boom, the less impressive their performance is likely to be. In fact the economics of Florida's theories look good only if you take a snapshot of the numbers in a narrow time range—just before the Internet bubble burst.

It's no mystery why the numbers turn out this way. Florida's basket of indexes selects cities that participated in that bubble. The professor focused on these cities in developing his theories: it was their characteristics that he sought to identify when he constructed his various creativity indexes, so it's predictable that they wound up scoring highest. Florida's entire theory, in other words, is based on circular logic.

Jobs don't tell the whole story. Florida likes to talk about his most creative cities as centers of innovation, and, based on his writings, one would assume that these cities would be home to thousands of fast-growing companies.

But many are not. In fact, according to one recent independent study of entrepreneurship in America, Florida's most creative cities are no more likely to be powerful incubators of fast-growing businesses than those at the bottom of his rankings.

In 2001 a National Commission on Entrepreneurship study entitled Mapping America's Entrepreneurial Landscape ranked U.S. cities on how well they hatch high-growth companies. Unlike Florida, the commission developed a precise method of measuring high-growth centers: it calculated the percentage of companies in a local economy that grew by 15 percent a year for five consecutive years in the mid-1990s. Unlike Florida's anecdotal observations of places where he assumes that plenty of entrepreneurial activity is taking place, the commission's numbers-oriented approach precisely charts America's entrepreneurial topography. Unexpectedly, the study concludes that "most fast-growing, entrepreneurial companies are not in high tech industries" but are rather "widely distributed across all industries."

Among major cities, Detroit—omitted from Florida's most creative cities—finished second in the commission's report, incubating about 50 percent more fast-growing companies than the average of all major cities, with a particular strength in nurturing high-growth manufacturing businesses. By contrast, New York, which is among Florida's most creative big cities, finished at the bottom of the commission's study, producing fast-growing companies at less than half the rate of all big cities. The results were much the same for midsize cities. While Florida-favorite Austin scored well, finishing Number One among midsize cities, Las Vegas also shone, coming in second, despite ranking as one of Florida's least creative cities. Other inconsistencies abound. San Diego, perennially one of Florida's top-ranked cities, scores way below average in producing fast-growing companies, while Grand Rapids, Michigan, one of Florida's least creative cities, was well above average. The study demonstrates how Florida's theories aren't even good at predicting the most fundamental measure of entrepreneurship.

If Florida's cities can't produce jobs or high-growth companies at a rapid rate, you'd think they would at least do a good job of attracting and retaining people, given the professor's notion of the importance of place in the new economy, as a magnet not just for the talented but for residents of all kinds. But Florida is wrong again. Many of his "talent magnets" are among the worst at attracting and, more important, hanging on to residents. Just look at the 2000 Census reports on domestic migration, which follow the movements into and out of metro areas by U.S. residents. That report found that New York, among Florida's top talent magnets, lost 545,000 more U.S. residents than it gained in the latter half of the 1990s, the worst performance of any U.S. city. The greater San Francisco metro area was close behind, with a negative domestic migration of more than 200,000 people. In fact, five of the ten places atop Florida's Creativity Index had steep losses of U.S. residents during that period, while some of Florida's creative losers—including Las Vegas, Memphis, and Tampa Bay—were big winners.

The only thing that keeps some of Florida's "ideal" cities from population loss is that they attract large numbers of foreign immigrants, who replace fleeing U.S. citizens. But cities that operate this way can hardly be called talent magnets or economic engines, because the U.S. residents they lose are, by and large, better educated and wealthier than the immigrants they attract. To illustrate: an Empire Foundation study of New York City's out-migration during the mid-1990s found that those leaving Manhattan earned, on average, about $60,000 a year, while studies of IRS data have shown that foreign immigrants who move into New York typically earn just $25,000 their first year here, which puts them among the city's lowest 25 percent of earners.

It's no coincidence that some of Florida's urban exemplars perform so unimpressively on these basic measures of growth. As Florida tells us repeatedly, these cities spend money on cultural amenities and other frills, paid for by high taxes, while restricting growth through heavy regulation. Despite Florida's notion of a new order in economic development, the data make crystal-clear that such policies aren't people- or business-friendly. The 2000 Census figures on out-migration, for instance, show that states with the greatest loss of U.S. citizens in 1996 through 2000—in other words, the go-go years—have among the highest tax rates and are the biggest spenders, while those that did the best job of attracting and retaining people have among the lowest tax rates. A study of 1990 census data by the Cato Institute's Stephen Moore found much the same thing for cities. Among large cities, those that lost the most population over a ten-year period were the highest-taxing, biggest-spending cities in America, with per capita taxes 75 percent higher than the fastest-growing cities. Given those figures, maybe Florida should have called his book "The Curse of the Creative Class."

The city that sits at the pinnacle of Florida's list, often jokingly referred to as the "People's Republic of San Francisco" because of its socialistic political culture, is the perfect example of what happens to cities that follow this heavy-handed governing philosophy. While San Francisco sports taxes higher than all but a few U.S. cities and passes laws forcing business to boost wages, San Francisco's jobs economy has expanded at only one-fourth the rate of the national economy over the last twenty years. Similarly, high-tax New York has been caught in a cycle of boom and bust that has produced no net job growth in forty years. During the mid-1990s the city briefly got back to basics when the Giuliani administration focused on fighting crime and cutting some taxes and spending, and—presto!—for the longest period since World War II, the city's economy outpaced the nation's. Now that the city's political culture has veered sharply to the left again, with a mayor who declares that taxes don't matter to businesses or residents, New York is once again an economic slacker.

These examples only accentuate what is otherwise obvious: there is little evidence that people or businesses set much store on what Florida is prescribing. A *Money* magazine poll rating dozens of factors that people consider in choosing a place to live found that the top ten reasons fell into two broad categories: low costs (including low property and sales taxes) and basic quality-of-life issues (good schools, low crime, clean air and water). By contrast, such Florida-esque issues as diversity ranked twenty-second on the list, while cultural amenities such as theaters and museums ranked twenty-seventh and lower, and outdoor activities still lower.

The *Money* list illustrates an underlying problem with Florida's whole approach. Not only does he believe that marginal attractions such as an idiosyncratic arts scene can build economic power; he thinks that government officials and policymakers like himself can figure out how to produce those things artificially. He doesn't seem to recognize that the cultural attributes of the cities he most admires are not a product of government planning but have been a spontaneous development, financed by private-sector wealth. While Florida's writings denigrate efforts of cities to power their economies by building sports stadiums and convention centers, the professor thinks that he, by contrast, has found the philosopher's stone that will turn public spending on amenities into economic-development gold.

It is exactly because Florida is an exponent of this kind of aggressive, government-directed economic development (albeit with a New Age spin) that liberal policymakers and politicians have latched on to his theories so enthusiastically. To them, an expanding government is always more interesting than an expanding economy—especially if economic growth depends on something so very uninteresting as low taxes and small government. But it is just as likely that the Floridazed brand of aggressive governing will get things as wrong as the builders of sports stadiums and convention centers.

One clear example of how things are likely to go wrong is in Richmond, Virginia, where the city fathers and local economic-development types—touting Florida's ideas—tried to revive their downtown by making it a trendy arts district. To finance its efforts, the town recently passed a restaurant tax and is now contemplating raising its hotel taxes—to the howls of local businesses. "They haven't figured out that those tax increases will probably kill as many jobs as their plan will create," says Scott Moody, a senior economist with the Tax Foundation.

If Richmond's city leaders have their priorities askew, they are not alone in the creative age. Concerned with inessentials, cities under Florida's thrall can easily overlook what residents really want. Consider Winnipeg's former mayor Glen Murray, one of Canada's chief Florida fans, who even brought the professor north to tout his ideas to Canadian political leaders. While Murray invested in cultural amenities and derided people who only want cities to focus on "pipes, pavement and policing," the most distinguishing characteristic of Murray's mayoralty was this: for several consecutive years, Winnipeg was the murder capital of Canada.

Welcome to the creative age.

. . . .

SIX

Who Really Runs New York?

In the fall of 2003, New York mayor Michael Bloomberg engineered a campaign to replace New York's party primary elections with a form of nonpartisan elections in which candidates don't run on party lines. Bloomberg touted this election reform—a nostrum first advanced by the Progressive reformers at the beginning of the twentieth century—as a way to weaken the party bosses in New York and thus, in his description, open up public office to energetic and capable candidates, much like himself, who are not creatures of a party.

Bloomberg's effort, which was resoundingly defeated at the ballot box in November 2003, was useful only insofar as it cast an especially bright light on the way that New York's politics have changed over the years. Stuck in a time warp, Bloomberg seemed to think that New York was still living in the days when Tammany Hall bigwigs like

Carmine DeSapio or Boss Tweed chose candidates based on party loyalty, without regard to merit or local support, and when energetic Republicans like Fiorello La Guardia battled the party bosses by constructing fusion tickets of reform-minded voters.

But New York City's political system, like that of many cities across America, has been utterly transformed since those days. Now, instead of party bosses running city hall, it is powerful public-employee unions and community non-profit groups living off government money that control the city's political process and political agenda, often at the expense of the city's taxpayers and businesses. While these groups are aligned with the Democratic party, they are not subservient to the party; the party has become their instrument, a tool of their convenience.

The movement that reshaped New York politics—eroding the power of party bosses and paving the way for greater influence of public-sector factions—began in the mid-1950s when an alliance of middle-class Jewish Democrats and the WASP elite, led by the likes of Herbert Lehman and Eleanor Roosevelt, worked to unseat the Irish and Italian conservative Democrats who ran Tammany Hall. These chieftains had long wielded power through a network of neighborhood political clubs that served as the eyes and ears of the party and provided useful services to constituents, from getting a traffic light fixed, to lobbying for a new neighborhood school, to bringing complaints of local businesses to the attention of city hall. In return, the club expected constituents' loyalty on Election Day. The clubs also were the conduit through which the party machines dispensed patronage, with each club generally granted rights to several dozen city jobs at any one time, which the head of the club gave out as rewards to successful district leaders and their relatives.

When the reformers ousted the last Tammany boss, Carmine DeSapio, in 1961 and systematically attacked the machines in other boroughs, the neighborhood political clubs began disappearing, leaving a void in many communities, which the reformers showed little interest in filling. "Liberals are not neighborhood people," wrote Daniel Patrick Moynihan about the transformation of the Democratic party in the city after Tammany's demise.

Into the vacuum stepped several new-style groups that rapidly accumulated political power but had a very different agenda from that of the neighborhood clubs, an agenda that focused on bigger government, more spending, and ultimately higher taxes. One new power appeared in the form of unions representing public-sector employees, who won the right to organize in New York City in 1954 and to bargain collectively with the city in 1958. Almost immediately the unions began throwing their weight around, demanding higher wages and better benefits and work rules, and within a decade they had staged a series of debilitating strikes against Gotham to achieve these goals.

Government-employee union leaders quickly saw that political power was essential to their success: elections were a way for them to pick their members' bosses and to influence who would sit across the bargaining table from them. They began mobilizing heavily in support of candidates who pledged to protect their interests; and soon that era's union leaders—men like Victor Gotbaum of District Council 37 and Albert Shanker of the teachers' union—became political heavyweights and kingmakers. So successful were these groups that by the mid-1960s, political scientist Theodore Lowi observed that the public-employee bureaucracy in New York was emerging as "the new machine."

This modern Tammany Hall introduced a new kind of patronage that proved far more destructive to the city than the type fostered by the original party machines. Even in Tammany's heyday, patronage accounted for only a few thousand municipal jobs. But with the rise of public unions—whose raison d'être was to boost their own membership, to protect workers' interests, and to thwart efforts at downsizing government or making it more efficient through privatization and other means—the city's workforce numbers bolted upward and continued on that arc with only brief interruptions for over forty years, so that today New York's government employs about 100,000 more workers than it did in the mid-1960s, a 30 percent increase, while its population has remained essentially unchanged.

Not long after public-sector unions became a force, another new political power arose in neighborhoods: government-funded, community-based social-services organizations. Spurred by Mayor John Lindsay's efforts to decentralize government, and lavishly funded with government dollars by President Lyndon Johnson's War on Poverty, activists formed organizations that built subsidized housing, ran day-care centers, and operated health clinics. From practically nothing in the early 1960s, by 1967 there were more than 400 federal grant programs providing $15 billion to these local groups around the country, with a heavy concentration in New York because of the influence of Mayor Lindsay, whom Washington policymakers touted as one of urban America's new leaders. Spurred by this government largesse, social-services organizations grew in New York City from a few hundred, employing fewer than 50,000 people in the mid-1960s, to more than 4,000 today, employing 185,000 people.

Over time these groups have become a new kind of neighborhood political clubhouse, running and successfully electing their own members to political office. Activists like Ramon Velez, who ran a network of social services agencies out of his base in Hunts Point in the Bronx, or Pedro Espada, Jr., who built a single health clinic in the Soundview section of the South Bronx into a sweeping public services empire, used the influence they gained in neighborhoods as a launching pad for political careers. And rather than focusing on ensuring that the neighborhood got clean streets, adequate policing, and good schools, the new clubhouses advanced a social welfare agenda more concerned with bringing the latest government-funded halfway house, drug treatment center, or job-training program to a neighborhood—to be run by Velezes, Espadas, and their counterparts, and staffed by loyal supporters— whether the community needed the service or not.

Today these community activists and government careerists dominate the politics of New York City in a way that borough bosses and the neighborhood political clubs of Tammany once did, making New York's public servants in effect the city's political masters. Working both within the Democratic party and outside it, they have created a coalition of public-sector interests—of tax eaters. Irrespective of the public interest, their interest is always more: more city workers with more pay, more social services, more pensions, more benefits—and more taxes.

You can see the extent of their dominance in the way these forces took advantage of the city's most recent election-law change, which instituted term limits. Although term limits were intended to open up the political process to outsiders, when the law went into effect in 2001 public-sector insiders and activists swarmed into the Democratic primary races. A perfect case in point is a city council race in a solidly middle-class black section of southeast Queens. The seven candidates who ran for the Democratic party nomination included two members of the United Federation of Teachers (one of whom was a union delegate), two professors at (unionized) city-run colleges, a former New York City high school principal, an assistant commissioner of the city's Parks Department, an executive at a publicly funded substance-abuse clinic (who was the local Democratic organization's candidate), and an administrator of a publicly funded welfare services organization, who ultimately prevailed against the party organization's candidate.

The lineup was much the same throughout the city, so that nearly seven in ten of the newly elected city council members had backgrounds in government or in publicly funded social services. Moreover, in several crucial districts these new councilmen had trounced opponents backed by the Democratic party organization—belying the Bloomberg notion that a cabal of bosses runs the city.

Increasingly these days, public-sector candidates, nominally Democrats, are simply using the party as a flag of convenience. Nothing illustrates more clearly how the Democratic party has become the tail on the public-sector dog than a 2003 Democratic primary in the Bronx, pitting two social-services powerhouses against each other. The battle took place in Soundview, ruled for years by Pedro Espada Jr., one of the earliest of the social-services kingpins.

Espada's publicly funded empire of health-care clinics and programs for welfare mothers and senior citizens, serving about 100,000 residents a year, made him one of the most recognized figures in the community and helped both him and his son get elected to various public offices, at first with the support of the Democratic party but later as rebels, powerful and independent enough to thumb their noses at the party.

After several unsuccessful efforts by the Bronx Democratic party to oust the renegade Espadas, the family recently suffered a crushing defeat at the hands of another power within the social-services community, the Local 1199 health-care workers' union. Sensing an opportunity to defeat Espada's son in a city council race because more than four thousand members of 1199 live in the district, one of the union's organizers, Annabel Palma, enlisted the support of her bosses and other union activists for her candidacy and then leveraged that into an endorsement from the Democratic party. The move left young Espada complaining, understandably if inaccurately, that the party was "hiring" a union to defeat him. Union members helped pour over $90,000 in contributions into their candidate's war chest, a hefty sum for a first-time city council candidate, and hundreds of health-care workers fanned out across the district to support her bid. "[She] has a million foot soldiers out there with 1199," Bronx state assembly member Rubén Díaz marveled. The result was a smashing victory for the union-backed candidate in an election in which the official Democratic party's support was largely inconsequential and almost an afterthought.

The Democratic party, as these recent elections make clear, is hardly the all-powerful force that the mayor and other nonpartisan-election fans believe it is. In fact, if there is a significant overarching force behind the city's public-sector politics today, it is the Working Families party—which, with fewer than seven thousand registered voters, is not at all a political party in the conventional sense. Rather, it is a union instrument of electoral politics, mobilizing the membership of its affiliated public-sector unions and union-boosting activist groups like ACORN to support its preferred candidates, as in the Palma–Espada race. Using New York State's unusual election law, which allows minor parties to endorse candidates from other parties, the WFP has been able to work both with the Democratic leadership and at times against it to elect candidates hewing to its agenda of bigger government and higher taxes.

This strategy has worked smoothly. In 2001, for instance, nineteen candidates endorsed for various municipal offices by the WFP won their Democratic primary elections—with several of the victories coming at the expense of candidates backed by the Democratic party's official county organizations—and then went on to win the general election. In the city council, where fifteen WFP-backed candidates won, those victories gave the WFP the kind of voting bloc that no other minor party has ever had. The WFP has used that new voting power to introduce and pass an array of significant legislation in the new council, some of it over the mayor's veto, including an expansion of the city's living-wage laws and the toughest predatory lending bill in the country. The party's success, smacking of *The Invasion of the Body Snatchers*, has prompted even the *New York Times* to note that the WFP has emerged as "a significant policy-making force," an extraordinary statement about a "party" with a tiny handful of registered members.

More and more Democratic candidates are now recognizing the WFP's power. Up to thirty Democratic city council incumbents sought and received the WFP's endorsement for the 2003 elections. That has given the WFP a majority on the city council, which, if recent history is any guide, it will use with more purpose and effectiveness than the Democratic party has used its majority to push legislatively for the party agenda of higher taxes—including a stock-transfer tax and a wealth tax on rich New Yorkers—an expansion of the city's union-strengthening living-wage law to cover more workers, and a greater burdening of city businesses with still more regulations and requirements.

What Mayor Bloomberg didn't understand is that an electoral reform like nonpartisan voting would do nothing to mitigate the power of the Working Families party, which is merely the political face of the public-sector unions. It might actually increase the political influence of the WFP and its pro-union activist allies. That's because any switch to nonpartisan voting, by eliminating party primaries, would further weaken the ability of already weak Democratic county bosses to select candidates and sway elections. When that happens, as the experience of nonpartisan voting in other cities demonstrates, other well-established groups will fill the void.

While in some cities that group could be a business or civic organization—as in Dallas, where a business group has elected fifteen of the last seventeen mayors under nonpartisan voting—in cities like New York, where business or taxpayer-led civic groups are weak and ineffective, it is the public-sector-oriented organizations that benefit. "In New York City, groups like unions, politically active churches, and community organizations would dominate in a nonpartisan environment," says Ted Arrington, professor of political science at the University of North Carolina–Charlotte and a longtime observer of nonpartisan voting. These groups, after all, have all the necessary infrastructure of a political party: a strong organization, a host of workers to campaign and get out the vote, and the ability to raise money—as well as a powerful motive of self-interest.

What New York politics needs today is not more electoral reform but a viable two-party system that offers taxpayers and private-sector employers candidates who will represent their interests against the overwhelming political clout of the public-sector special interests that have become the New Left in many cities. Such voters made themselves heard in the city's mayoral elections of 1993, 1997, and 2001, when candidates running on the Republican line assembled a classic coalition of outer-borough, ethnic, middle-class voters—the kind who used to be the soul of Gotham's Democratic party before it veered sharply left— and used it to defeat candidates heavily backed by public-sector unions and community activist groups. But no one, not former mayor Rudy Giuliani or Bloomberg or the state GOP's leadership, has made any effort to assemble that coalition permanently. In numerous districts throughout the city where both Giuliani and Bloomberg won handily, candidates representing the tax-eaters' agenda have triumphed in city council or state legislature races because they ran without taxpayer-interest opposition.

Although the odds against creating such an effective organization to represent taxpaying interests seem steep, the numbers give hope. In the 2001 mayoral election, for example, 48 percent of Hispanics voted for GOP candidate Bloomberg, up from the hefty 43 percent they gave GOP candidate Giuliani four years earlier. In a *New York Times* poll taken in 2003, black and Hispanic voters were even less favorably disposed toward higher taxes and more inclined to demand that public-sector workers do more to help solve the city's budget crisis, than were white voters—an indication that the city's growing minority middle class is ripe for something other than the public-sector-oriented candidates now dominating the landscape. A party advocating in every city race the proven urban agenda that revived New York in the 1990s—fiscal restraint, effective policing, and school choice—could begin to present an alternative to the public-sector domination of the city.

. . . .

SEVEN

A Council of Dunces

What was the New York city council concerned about in early January 2002, when a municipal budget crisis loomed, the economy foundered, and downtown residents and workers still struggled to get back to normalcy four months after the terrorist attacks?

The art on the walls.

Yup, art: no sooner was former Black Panther Charles Barron sworn in as one of thirty-eight new council members than he announced that high on his agenda would be ensuring that the portraits of famous figures in municipal buildings depicted more "people of color." Barron was echoing the sentiments of a council colleague, Philip Reed, who had complained, "When I look at the pictures, the first thing that strikes me is how few women there are." Such concerns, explained incoming councilman Al Vann, "exemplified the new spirit" of the new council, which wasted the next few weeks trying to get a painting of the city's first black mayor, David Dinkins, hung in a prominent place in the council chambers.

The agitation over art set the keynote for New York's new and zany city council, which is the perfect expression of the new political system that has been emerging in cities like New York, where politics are now dominated by powerful public-sector interests. The depressing result of those new politics are daily on display in the New York city council, which has been by turns comic and trivial, inflammatory and divisive, and almost always destructive. With a veto-proof majority in its Democratic caucus, the council has proved as unfriendly to business as it is unsympathetic to taxpayers. It has pumped out a wide array of legislation aimed at rolling back many of the Giuliani-era reforms that uplifted the city during the 1990s. Nothing so threatens the future of New York as a radicalized city council free to work its will without restraint.

The new city council is the unintended consequence of two policy changes that at first seemed harmless. In 1989 a court decision forced Gotham to dismantle the Board of Estimate, the body that previously held much of the power over city budget and land issues, and invest more power in the city council. What had until then been a nearly irrelevant legislature—once described by former parks commissioner Henry Stern as not even a rubber stamp, "because a stamp at least leaves an impression"—suddenly moved to the center of the city's decision-making process. As the council's power began to grow in the early 1990s, a circle of outer-borough members representing middle-income districts, led by Majority Leader Peter Vallone, determined to chart a fiscally restrained course on taxes and spending, and the council that emerged under charter reform steered clear of embarrassing imbroglios, at least most of the time.

But the landscape changed radically when New Yorkers adopted a second innovation: in a 1993 referendum they approved term limits that would force a majority of incumbent council members to step down in 2001. For years until 2001, the character of New York politics had been slowly evolving, as the old neighborhood political clubs and borough organizations that had produced many candidates disappeared or waned in power, replaced by municipal-worker unions, social-services organizations, and powerful community-based housing and economic-development groups, all dependent on government funding. But the evolution became a revolution in November 2001 when political activists scored big victories in city council elections, changing the council's ideological character overnight. Almost a third of the winners ran with endorsements from the Working Families party, the essentially socialist third party founded by organizers from left-wing unions and radical community groups like ACORN, for whom New York's liberal Democratic party was too conservative. Nearly 70 percent of the new councilmen had backgrounds in government, social services, or community activism—people like Gale Brewer, once chief of staff to former left-wing Manhattan borough president Ruth Messinger, or Robert Jackson of the New York State Public Employees Federation. Higher-profile new councilmen of the same stamp include Al Vann, notorious for heading the racist African-American Teachers Association in the 1960s, when it clashed with white teachers during the Ocean Hill–Brownsville school decentralization crisis; Bill de Blasio, Hillary Clinton's 2000 campaign manager; and Eric Gioia, Al Gore's New York campaign manager in 2000.

A startling example of the council's leftward drift is David Weprin, a former municipal-finance banker whose experience on Wall Street and as a corporate lawyer seems not to jibe with his tax-and-spend politics. Weprin, who represents middle-income neighborhoods in Queens, is a bundle of contradictions only possible in New York. He fits the profile of the classic moderate New York Democrat, like his predecessor, Herb Berman, who frequently fought to keep a lid on taxes in the city. But Weprin, the son of former State Assembly leader Saul Weprin, ran with the support of the Working Families party and hasn't disappointed them. He was among the first councilmen to push for tax hikes—even castigating Mayor Bloomberg for not proposing more tax increases in his first budget. He has offered a raft of his own new taxes, including a surcharge on wealthy New Yorkers. He opposed President Bush's proposed dividend tax cut—which boosted the city's securities industry and thereby bolstered the municipal budget—because he would rather see "direct assistance" from Washington to New York. This is a rather startling position for someone who once served as chairman of the Securities Industry Association, Wall Street's most powerful lobbying group, which strongly supported the dividend tax cut. But it's typical for the political culture of New York, which shows more interest in handouts from the state and federal governments than in cultivating budgetary self-reliance and private-sector job growth in Gotham.

Worsening the problem with the new council is that Majority Leader Gifford Miller changed the way the body runs, setting in place a laissez-faire regime that has unleashed the most extreme elements. A young Upper East

Sider with big political ambitions, Miller left no doubt as to where he stands on the ideological spectrum: he was inspired to enter politics by Bill Clinton's election, he says—a relief to him after the Age of Reagan. "I was no fan of Reagan," Miller pronounced to the *New York Times Magazine*. "There is a certain politics of greed that I reject." Miller went to work for Upper East Side congresswoman Carolyn Maloney—among the farthest left of the city's congressional delegation—and then won election to the city council seat vacated when Republican Charles Millard joined the Giuliani administration.

To win the speaker's job, Miller had to promise to depart from the way the council operated under Vallone, who tightly controlled its agenda and its members. After the November 2001 elections, several newly elected councilmen who dubbed themselves the "Fresh Democracy Council" demanded more power for council committees to set their own platforms and more freedom for individual members to push their interests. Seeking their support, Miller declared, "The next speaker needs to be the type of leader who brings more empowerment to council members and forms a team which represents meaningful consultation."

And who was Miller empowering when he reached out to Fresh Democracy? One of those instrumental in the group was ex–Black Panther Barron, who emerged as an agent provocateur of the new council, especially on racial matters, using his perch to promote an increasingly angry and divisive agenda, usually with barely a word of dissent from his colleagues. Miller's governing style empowers Barron's antics. As Barron himself says in praise of Miller's rule: "I am able to be as radical—to be black as I want to be."

Just a few months after taking office, Barron garnered headlines by telling a rally on slavery reparations that sometimes he felt he wanted to "slap" a white person for the sake of his own mental health. A soft-spoken man whose grandfatherly tone often belies the venom of his message, Barron embarrassed the city further when he threw a council reception for Zimbabwean tyrant Robert Mugabe. As chair of the council's committee on higher education—a juicy assignment that Speaker Miller handed him—Barron held a hearing tinged with racist overtones on Governor Pataki's proposed tuition hikes at the City University of New York. "We used to have free tuition," Barron declared. "Then, when the complexion of the university changed, we had tuition." He sat respectfully, along with a host of equally encouraging council members, as students testifying before his committee made increasingly hysterical and inflammatory remarks, with one student at Medgar Evers College declaring that the tuition increases "were a calculated effort to prevent people like me or other brown-skin people from getting an education."

While Barron's antics have gotten headlines, the quiet machinations of the rest of the new council have been much more destructive. With unions and activists setting its agenda, the new council became virulently anti-business, threatening the economic future of the city. Bills that the council has already passed have worsened the business climate in what is already one of the country's most heavily taxed, heavily regulated cities—a city still struggling to recover from a severe downturn in its Number One industry and a terrorist attack on its Number Two business district.

Taking its orders from the Working Families party—and especially from ACORN—the council quickly passed a

123

"living-wage" bill, setting a new minimum wage more than three dollars above the federal minimum for many private companies that do business with the city. The debate over the living wage produced the kind of tortured logic now typical of the council. For instance, Wall Street veteran Weprin, who should know better, argued that the council had to enact a living-wage bill to ensure that low-wage workers had enough money to pay for a property-tax increase that the council recently had approved, as if the city council could simply ordain that the private sector in New York generate more wages for workers to use in paying higher taxes.

Even though New York City now has fifty thousand workers under living-wage legislation, more than any other U.S. city, living-wage supporters are not satisfied. When the council reduced the bill's scope in response to Bloomberg administration complaints that the original legislation would cost city hall itself $100 million annually, the sponsors vowed to seek a wider law later on. "We're going to come back with a bigger net," said Deputy Majority Leader Bill Perkins.

The new council seems intent on doing the bidding of its most radical union supporters through the narrowest special-interest legislation. At the same time the council sent the mayor the living-wage legislation, to take only one further example, it also passed a bill that forces the new buyer of a building to keep the previous maintenance and security staff employed for up to ninety days and then provide written evaluations of each employee. To fire workers, the owner must then go through an arduous arbitration process. Although the council claims that it was trying to create "stability" in the workforce, the legislation is an unprecedented intrusion on employer-employee relations and was a direct gift to the powerful local union that represents building workers—and that pushed for the law. The law allows unionized buildings to opt out of the burdensome employee retention and evaluation process, a clear incentive for the new owner to unionize the workforce rather than deal with the consequences of the legislation. "The old city council certainly had union interests at heart," says Joseph Strasburg, formerly Peter Vallone's chief of staff and now president of the Rent Stabilization Association, a landlord group, "but at least the old council wasn't a wholly owned subsidiary of the unions."

The displaced-worker bill shows the council at its most cynical. When the Bloomberg administration objected that the original bill could cost the city millions of dollars, presumably in administrative and compliance costs, the council simply changed the legislation to exclude city-owned buildings. But in its report on the legislation, the council nevertheless asserted, in clear contradiction to this action, that the bill would add no significant costs to the private sector.

Other council legislation makes clear that the members care little for the long-term effects of their measures, so long as they can claim short-term victories. "These members will be gone in eight years," says Strasburg of the Rent Stabilization Association, "so they don't seem worried that they will have to deal with the consequences of their actions." One example of how term limits have shortened the body's time horizon is a bill that targets predatory lenders. On its surface the bill seems like a worthwhile effort to curb abusive practices among lending companies that charge excessive fees on mortgages and home equity loans to poor, inner-city residents, or that make the loans expecting to seize the homes when borrowers fall behind in payments. But the council law, stricter than any other in the nation, contains a number of provisions that threaten to dry up capital for all high-interest loans, most of which represent legitimate lending to people with poor credit.

The law targets financial institutions that purchase mortgages in bulk from lending companies and package them into securities, a practice that provides an essential stream of capital to the mortgage market. The New York City law makes these financial institutions liable if any genuinely predatory loans (as opposed to merely high-interest loans) wind up as part of their portfolios, even though these institutions have no way of knowing what transpires between a borrower and lender, or whether the lender complied with all laws in making the loan. The law attempts to punish these mortgage packagers by barring them from doing business with New York City government, a hefty price to pay for those financial institutions that New York uses as bond underwriters and pension fund managers. Financial industry experts have warned that, rather than lose that lucrative business, some big firms may get out of the market of buying up loans, depriving lenders of capital to make fresh loans to the 90-plus percent of struggling high-credit-risk borrowers who ultimately succeed in repaying their mortgages.

These bills, favorites of activists and union groups, went nowhere in the previous council. That they have now become law has spurred activists to resurrect a host of more damaging legislation. They have already proposed bills that would impose commercial rent control—a move that could devastate the commercial market in the city in the same way that more than 50 years of residential rent control has constricted the city's housing stock. Other bills would force government contractors to ensure that at least half their workforce on municipal jobs reside in the five boroughs; would ban companies that profited in any way from slavery over 150 years ago from doing business with the city today; and would resurrect the city's affirmative-action contracting program, which gives a 10 percent price advantage to minority firms in competitive bidding, at a time of huge budget deficits, even though the 1990s witnessed unprecedented growth in the city's minority business community without any such contracting program in place.

A council so cavalier about the city's business environment is also a council intent on pumping up the city's already high tax rates to finance its members' many schemes. When Mayor Bloomberg was briefly trying to hold the line against new taxes, nearly half the councilmen signed on to an agenda—essentially drafted by the Working Families party—that called for a wide array of new taxes, including reestablishing a tax on stock transactions at a time when Wall Street was already in a deep recession. The council has also called for a personal income-tax surcharge on wealthy individuals, to finance increases in the Board of Education's $12 billion budget. When the mayor then proposed a property-tax increase, the council approved it in just a few days, with no public hearings. "In New York City, when somebody sneezes we hold council hearings. But for the biggest tax increase in the city's history, we held no hearings," complains Queens councilman Anthony Avella, one of only three Democrats to vote against the property-tax hike.

Avella says he opposed the increase because the council jumped to close the budget gap with higher taxes, without seriously weighing spending cuts. But Avella was also one of the few Democrats in the city who faced a serious election challenge from a Republican, and he is likely to face a tough reelection too. To punish Avella's apostasy, Speaker Miller took away his seat on one of the council's committees and justified doing so by saying that the council had to speak with a unified voice to be effective—exactly the opposite of the position he took in giving members of the Fresh Democracy Council and other supporters free rein to pursue their agendas. (The three Republicans on the fifty-one-member council, who all opposed the tax increases, faced similar intimidation from Mayor Bloomberg, their party's putative leader.)

Despite the council's track record, many of its most liberal members reject the notion that it is anti-business or that their constituents vehemently opposed the property-tax increases. Weprin says the council took the concerns of the business community into consideration and modified the living-wage and displaced-worker legislation accordingly. He adds that the council reduced the mayor's property-tax increase to 18.5 percent from 25 percent—though the council proposed a host of other taxes too. And Leroi Comrie, representing a predominantly black Queens district with one of the highest concentrations of single-family homes in the city, argues that his constituents favored higher taxes over reduced services.

Some critics believe that, now that so much political power is concentrated in the hands of a few activist groups, many council members no longer attend meetings of local civic and homeowner associations, where there is plenty of anger about the property-tax hike. Says Corey Bearak, executive vice president of the Queens Civic Congress:

"Instead, they are going to meetings of these government-funded, community-based organizations, and they are hearing from these groups that they are happy the city has preserved their funding." Since these groups have inordinate power in the Democratic primaries, currying their favor remains key. "City Hall is filled with lobbyists for every program imaginable, but there is no lobbyist for the middle class in New York City," laments Republican councilman Dennis Gallagher.

Of course some council members make no pretense at all of favoring a business-friendly New York. Businessmen and taxpayers who want a glimpse of what's ahead for the city should listen to what Councilman Barron thinks about managing the city's economy. "We're making the city friendlier to poor people, to working people, to people in need," he avers. "It's not about greed but about need in New York now. Maybe businesses won't make as much as they used to make in New York, but they'll at least be able to make a profit." Although Wall Street profits have been down from as much as $30 billion a few years ago, says Barron, firms in New York still earned $8 billion in 2002. "I don't think there will ever be a mass exodus of business from New York," Barron told *City Journal*, a statement that echoes similar pronouncements by other council members and the mayor but that contradicts the experience of the last thirty years, as banking and securities jobs, especially, streamed out of the city by the hundreds of thousands.

Although the council has its greatest impact on budgetary matters, new members are trying to radicalize a wide range of issues, from policing to social programs. The common theme of these efforts: working to undermine many of the Giuliani administration reforms that played such a big part in saving the city. One target of about a dozen council members, led by Barron and Deputy Majority Leader Perkins, is the New York Police Department. A series of bills introduced by these councilmen would strengthen the civilian complaint review board and give it the power to prosecute police officers. Another bill would ban racial or ethnic profiling by the Police Department, even though there is no evidence that the NYPD has ever engaged in either.

Similarly, the council has the Giuliani administration's welfare reforms in its sights. A proposed law would weaken the city's welfare-to-work program, allowing recipients to substitute education or job training for work, even though these programs have conclusively proved useless at getting recipients off welfare. Under Giuliani, welfare recipients declined from more than 1 million to under 500,000, in large part thanks to the welfare-to-work strategies that the council would subvert.

For good measure, the council seems intent on preventing some future Giuliani-style mayor, elected with strong support from the city's moderate voting blocs, from wielding as much power as Giuliani did. A proposed law, sponsored by nearly half the council, would amend the city charter to give the council veto power over most mayoral appointments, including all city commissioners. Such a law would allow a council increasingly filled with public-sector-oriented members to frustrate the designs of any mayor who was not its political ally.

When not preoccupied with playing the anti-Giuliani, the council regularly steps into matters over which it has neither power nor expertise. Councilmen have sparred over resolutions about Middle East policy, for instance. Members passed a resolution condemning President Bush and the Republicans for not expanding health-care benefits, and—like the legislatures of other left-of-center municipalities around America—passed a resolution opposing the war with Iraq. One sponsor of the resolution, Robert Jackson, complained that the measure took so long to approve because of opposition from New York's Jews.

All these antics could have political ramifications for years to come, because the council serves as the local political minor leagues, preparing candidates for higher office in New York. Speaker Miller has mayoral ambitions. Other council members, including Barron and Perkins, are already eyeing a spot in the city's congressional delegation, since members from their districts may well retire soon. Councilmen also often become public advocate or comptroller, stepping-stones to still higher office.

Nothing on the horizon promises to moderate the council's growing extremism anytime soon, unless the business owners, moderate and conservative politicians, and civic groups who have an interest in sensible and restrained government band together to change the council's makeup. But these groups often work against one another. To forestall property-tax increases, for instance, some homeowner groups recommended higher business taxes. Business organizations, meanwhile, often won't support Republican or moderate Democratic candidates because they believe they have little chance of winning—thereby creating a self-fulfilling prophecy. Even now, business groups alarmed by the council's leftward march are trying to assert their influence by donating more heavily to incumbents, a move that will only make those incumbents stronger.

Separately, none of these constituencies can master the forces that term limits unleashed on New York politics. But collectively they might jolt some sense into the council's increasingly self-destructive policies. If they don't hang together, they will hang separately, as the city experiences a torrent of anti-business, anti-taxpayer legislation that will damage it for years to come.

EIGHT

. . . .

The Antidote: A Free Market at Work

In College Point, Queens, immigrant Thomas Chen, a former apartment-building superintendent with little formal education, built a $40-million-a-year window-manufacturing business in less than ten years. In the South Bronx, Philson Warner, a Trinidadian immigrant, uses technology he developed as a researcher at Cornell University to run a commercial fish farm in the basement of an industrial building. In midtown Manhattan, Lloyd Grant, an ex-programmer at PaineWebber, scored success with a new business magazine aimed at the growing ranks of middle-class blacks not being served by traditional ethnic newspapers.

These three entrepreneurs, and thousands upon thousands like them from Flushing to Harlem, from Crow Hill to the South Bronx, from the Lower East Side to midtown, are part of the remarkable success story of minority business in New York City during the 1990s economic boom. By the end of 1997, according to the latest government five-year economic census, the city's 40,000 or so minority firms accounted for fully a quarter of all businesses in the city—employing more than 200,000 workers. Asians owned 24,000 of these businesses, Hispanics headed more than 9,100, and blacks ran nearly 5,700.

As part of this tidal wave of enterprise, another 197,000 minorities were self-employed sole proprietors. The ranks of Gotham's black sole proprietors increased by 76 percent from 1993 to 1997—compared with just 26 percent nationally. Local Latino entrepreneurs grew by 120 percent, compared with a 50 percent gain nationally. Today, after the record-breaking economic years of 1999 and 2000, the size of the minority business community is no doubt larger still.

The 400,000 jobs created by minority firms and sole proprietors accounted for 12 percent of New York's job base in 1997—which means that minorities didn't just benefit from the nineties boom but helped create it. Never before have minority businesses played so significant a role in Gotham or had such a stake in its future.

What's most striking is that this boom took place not because city government rolled out special programs for minority entrepreneurs or enacted even a smidgen of the "progressive" economic or social legislation called for by the New New Left. Instead, for one brief eight-year span under Mayor Rudy Giuliani, the city nourished the private-sector economy by paying attention to the basics—driving down crime to restore civil order, and cutting taxes. The resulting boom—in which New York's economy outpaced the national economy for the first time in decades—is a vivid reminder that urban health results from city governments doing the basics well and then allowing the marketplace to work its magic for everyone. No amount of government wage legislation or investment in the arts or social agendas masquerading as economic development could have produced for the vast majority of New Yorkers what the free market accomplished.

With its rich and varied culture, New York City has long had successful, and visible, minority businesses. But until recently, minority entrepreneurs confined themselves to a few predictable industries: Chinese restaurants and garment factories, for instance, or Korean greengroceries or Latino-owned bodegas. As omnipresent as these businesses have seemed, their impact on the local economy was limited. Two decades ago the federal government's economic census of minority firms counted just 4,500 black, Latino, and Asian businesses in New York City, employing only about 18,000 people—a mere 9 percent of 1997's total. Added to that were another 36,000 self-employed minorities. These 54,000 workers accounted for only 2.5 percent of the city's job base.

Since then, a revolution has taken place in the city's small-business community. Today's new minority entrepreneurs are not just more numerous but also more sophisticated than their predecessors. They are more likely to be in a cutting-edge, high-technology business or in a mainstream industry that draws on Gotham's strength as a center of finance, business services, and media. Mobilizing their now considerable experience as managers in the corporate world, the city's black, Latino, and Asian entrepreneurs have leaped beyond traditional minority industries and are opening ad agencies, consulting firms, graphic and design shops, and publishing ventures, to name just a few. They are also taking their expertise out beyond Manhattan's main business districts, capitalizing on their corporate know-how and the city's newfound prosperity to tap into new markets.

The time is rapidly passing when many of these firms might even be considered "ethnic" or "minority" enterprises, as government statistics classify them. Many are solidly part of the major industries that drive the New York economy. And more are certainly on the way, as the growing number of minorities who work in professional and managerial jobs enriches the talent pool of potential entrepreneurs. If the holy grail of social policy has been to integrate urban minorities fully into the economic and social mainstream, the fact that so many of these businesses are not "black businesses" or "Asian businesses" but just New York businesses is evidence that something momentous and deeply hopeful has happened in the past decade in Gotham, where the American dream has been coming true.

One of the city's hottest restaurant designers, Nancy Mah, a second-generation Chinese American, typifies the new corporate-bred minority entrepreneur. Mah gained valuable design experience working for Ark Restaurants, a publicly held Manhattan company, and later joined the prestigious Rockwell Group, where she helped fashion such restaurants as Michael Jordan's Steakhouse and Ruby Foo's in Times Square. In 1999, Mah, then thirty-seven, decided to capitalize on her growing reputation and open her own Manhattan-based shop. "In big companies, there can be a lot of layers that inhibit the creative process," she says, explaining her decision to strike out on her own.

A Tennessee native who studied design in Italy, Mah hardly fits the stereotype of the ethnic small-business owner. Although she was drawn to New York because of its large Chinese population, Mah is cultivating a reputation as a designer with a New York style, rather than as an Asian-American designer. Her latest work, for instance, includes a chain of small cafés in Japan dubbed Gramercy New York. "A lot of people have wanted to typecast me as an Asian-inspired designer, but that alone doesn't really define what I do," she says. And the fact that it seems silly and irrelevant to think of her company as a "minority" business is evidence of the magnitude of the success of so many minority entrepreneurs like her.

Some of Gotham's pioneering urban entrepreneurs are not only part of this new generation of upscale minority executives but are prospering by offering that generation a product it wants. Lloyd Grant and Cynthia Franklin, a husband-and-wife team who publish *The Kip Business Report* out of offices in Columbus Circle, typify this trend. They decided to transform the small resumé-writing business that Franklin, a former AOL Time Warner exec, had started in grad school into a publishing venture aimed at the New York area's fast-proliferating black corporate managers. The result was *Kip's*, a four-year-old glossy publication with a circulation of twelve thousand and a readership of forty thousand. "We felt that the local ethnic media have not kept pace as our market has moved into the middle class," says Grant, noting that blacks now head such top New York companies as Merrill Lynch, AOL Time Warner, and American Express. "Accountants, bankers, and so forth were being ignored, so we aimed *Kip's* for them," he says.

To tap this market, *Kip's* staff of four full-timers and ten freelancers serves up investment advice and profiles of new black entrepreneurs—like a recent one of former New York Knick Charles Smith, now head of a local technology firm—as well as in-depth stories about local black-owned businesses, including a recent long, close look at Harlem's troubled Carver Bank. "There's a new level of sophistication among urban entrepreneurs that has to be recognized," says Grant. "Many are corporate refugees, but even mom-and-pop shops are more sophisticated these days."

These savvier urban entrepreneurs are reaching out beyond Gotham's main business districts too. The migration of minority corporate refugees out of Manhattan has helped bolster the small-business revival that has brought renewed economic vitality to the city's outer-borough neighborhoods. The last government economic census counted nearly 3,000 minority firms in the Bronx, 7,400 in Brooklyn, and nearly 11,000 in Queens.

Sheila McQueen is part of this revival. She gained valuable managerial experience as an account supervisor at a big Manhattan telemarketing firm but got fed up with the long hours and extensive travel. "I figured if I had to work this hard, I could work for myself," she says. Looking for an opportunity, she remembered how her mother had gotten jobs for her, cleaning medical offices when she was a kid, as a way of helping her learn responsibility. McQueen, then in her thirties, set up a commercial cleaning enterprise, operating out of her mother's South Bronx basement. After building the business, called Scrub Clean, for two and a half years, she recently moved it into its own offices in a Bronx commercial building. Her staff of fourteen consists largely of workers she's found in her neighborhood, including several former welfare recipients encouraged by welfare reform to find jobs. "As long as someone is willing to work, I'm willing to train them," says McQueen. "When people can support themselves, it changes them." So among other successes, these entrepreneurs are helping transform the culture of minority neighborhoods.

Joe Rivera is another of those who gained experience in Manhattan but started his own business closer to home. While working as a supervisor at a big textile manufacturing firm and living in Manhattan, Rivera began looking for business opportunities for himself. He zeroed in on the large number of medical facilities in the New York area, including in his native Bronx, where health care is the Number One employer. The result was Pipette Technologies, a company that Rivera started, which calibrates the devices that deliver or extract extremely small amounts of liquid for precise medical testing. He moved back to the Bronx and opened the business in his home. Now, five years later, he has moved the company into commercial office space, and, as a major expansion, he is distributing a line of pipettes under his own brand name. Echoing McQueen, Rivera says of his decision to leave the corporate world: "If I'm going to be working sixty hours a week, it might as well be for myself."

Entrepreneurs like McQueen and Rivera have benefited from changes in the culture of big companies and big institutions like hospitals, which now increasingly outsource crucial work to small firms. In today's hotly competitive environment, most of these big outfits are color-blind in selecting vendors. "Race isn't a factor any more when companies go looking for small-business partners," says Neil Pariser, senior vice president of the South Bronx Overall Economic Development Corporation. "Now, rather, the question is: 'What can your business do for me? What can your product do for me?' Corporations want results."

While sophisticated new urban entrepreneurs are helping transform Gotham's business community, traditional forces—including immigration—have also reshaped the landscape. In the 1990s, for the first time in three decades, the city's population grew as the proportion of foreign-born New Yorkers increased to about 35 percent. That spurred enterprising immigrants to find ways to serve burgeoning ethnic populations with money to spend. Flushing Avenue in and around Bushwick in Brooklyn became known in the 1990s as the Tortilla Triangle because of its bakeries and food-processing plants, which now produce about 10 million tortillas a week for local consumption. Indians helped boost shopping districts in Astoria and Long Island City, where they opened 150 restaurants and stores in the second half of the 1990s alone. Guyanese entrepreneurs, meanwhile, started as many as 500 retail businesses and restaurants to serve the growing Caribbean community in and around the Richmond Hill section of Queens—an area that in the early 1990s was dotted with empty storefronts.

The new breed of savvy, well-trained minority entrepreneur has been quick to recognize business opportunities that might otherwise go unnoticed in these increasingly vibrant ethnic neighborhoods. Nothing illustrates that better than Philson Warner's fish farm in a South Bronx basement—a farm that supplies the growing demand for tilapia fish from local Asian and Caribbean restaurants. Warner had spent twenty-two years as a researcher at Cornell University, applying the principles of modern, high-tech agriculture to urban settings. Drawing on his experience raising tilapia on fish farms in South America years ago, Warner embarked on an effort to farm the breed in big indoor tanks. Four years ago he signed a licensing agreement with Cornell, allowing him to use his research commercially; then he invested $300,000 in an elaborate system of tanks and water filtration. His company, Inner City Oceans, is already producing about two thousand pounds a week of tilapia, also known as Saint Peter's Fish because it once abounded in the Sea of Galilee.

"This is the future of agriculture," says Warner, who next wants to move beyond the ethnic marketplace into the mainstream by raising striped bass and then opening a processing plant in the Bronx to go along with his farm. "About 80 percent of the world's food is produced in and around cities," he observes.

Few businesses have done a better job of capitalizing on opportunities presented by the city's changing population than VP Music, run by a family of Jamaican immigrants who created a powerhouse music business largely by serving the Caribbean community's taste for reggae. The business, which employs fifty people in its Queens facilities, is an offshoot of a record store that Vincent and Patricia Chin started in downtown Kingston, Jamaica, in 1958. In the late 1970s the family—immigrants to Jamaica from China a generation earlier—became worried about the island's political turmoil, so they came to New York to open an outlet. Slowly that record store on Jamaica Avenue, Queens, evolved into a distribution center, then a record label. Today VP produces fifty to sixty albums a year, serving reggae fans in New York and around the country, and it has become legendary as an independent in a world of big corporate players. In 1999, *Billboard* magazine voted VP the top reggae label. "If you want to be in this business, you need to be in New York," says Randy Chin, thirty-nine, an engineer by training who joined the family business six years ago and is now vice president of marketing. "It keeps you close to the pulse of the market being so close to the community."

Minority businesses have contributed to these neighborhood revivals by providing jobs for the newest New Yorkers. They often employ workers from their own group, and some of the most successful minority-owned businesses are also among the biggest employers in minority communities. Such employers often transfer skills that they've spent years learning to their neighborhoods—skills that would otherwise disappear in New York.

Mose Chest, for instance, spent forty years in New York's leather business, rising all the way to general manager of a big Manhattan leather apparel manufacturer. When the business was sold, he struck out on his own, opening a manufacturing plant two years ago in the South Bronx to make leather components for hats and caps. He staffed his factory with people from local job-training courses, including some welfare-to-work programs, and he taught them the fine art of leather making. "You can't find people who know how to do this already; everyone has to be trained," says Chest. "I hire people who want to work and are willing to learn," he explains, voicing a sentiment that countless employers express—a sentiment that the most successful job-training programs have made their credo. Chest's company, C&S Leather Products, is part of the answer to the question of where welfare clients will find jobs. Such companies help create the virtuous circle of neighborhood economic, social, and cultural renewal that is under way in New York.

Indeed, many of these entrepreneurs feel that they are helping to transmit the American dream from themselves to others in their communities. Thomas Chen, the founder of Crystal Door and Window in College Point, Queens, came to America and got a job as an apartment-building superintendent when he found he couldn't stand working in a Chinese restaurant. He started making and installing window bars and gates during the late 1980s, when crime in the city was spiraling out of control. Soon he had a thriving side business, and in 1990 he opened Crystal with just a handful of employees. Today the firm employs 250 production workers in a 210,000-square-foot facility in Queens and is well known in the local Chinese community as a reliable employer. Many of the plant's workers have moved into neighboring Flushing to be near the factory. "Most of our workers are immigrants, and many have been with us almost from the beginning," says Chen. "They are extremely loyal."

Although this 1990s entrepreneurial boom is a pure product of the free market, government policies nevertheless permitted it to take off, just as they aborted it in the 1980s—and the contrast between the two eras is an instructive one for policymakers to consider now. In the devastating recession of the late 1980s, when small neighborhood establishments were already struggling, government hikes in business taxes and fees to close budget gaps sent firms of all types reeling, and the Dinkins administration further crushed small businesses by burying them under a mountain of tickets for commercial violations. Spurred on by high quotas, inspectors from the sanitation, consumer affairs, and fire departments blitzed neighborhood businesses, collecting an additional $20 million in fines and fees in fiscal 1992 alone.

These tickets added a sometimes crushing price to the cost of doing business, especially for neighborhood retailers. For instance, every sanitation violation for an empty bottle of Night Train Express dropped by a passing derelict in front of a store brought a $50 fine, and after a dozen violations, the fine quadrupled to $200. At one point the Small Business Congress, a lobbying group formed to protest the blitz, counted more than 100 Korean grocers paying $200 per ticket. This shakedown sparked bitterness among stores struggling to survive; storeowners wondered if the city even wanted them.

The overall effect on small business was ruinous. In 1991 alone, evictions of small firms for nonpayment of rent doubled. Not surprisingly, minority business growth slowed appreciably. From 1987 to 1992 the number of minority firms in Gotham grew by just 20 percent, less than half the national gain—and much of New York's paltry increase came from new Asian businesses serving the city's growing Chinese and Korean communities. By contrast, the city's tiny black-owned business community—just 2,371 firms employing 8,779 people—actually shrank under Dinkins, even though the city's first black mayor provided special support to them in the form of micro-loans, special grants, and set-aside programs that gave minority firms a 10 percent price advantage when bidding for city contracts.

The Giuliani administration took a far different approach, focusing on broader policies that supported the overall economy, like tax cuts and public safety, rather than relying on programs aimed at particular groups. Mayor Giuliani reversed the city's course on taxes—cutting key levies, including some crucial to small business, like the unincorporated business tax, the sales tax on clothing, and the tax on commercial rents, which reduced rents by 4.25 percent everywhere except in Manhattan's main business districts.

Giuliani had proclaimed that his most important economic tool would be to lower crime in the city, a policy crucial to the economic revival in the outer boroughs, where the drug trade had ravaged retail strips, and theft, muggings, and vandalism had drained the life out of manufacturing zones. A 1989 study found that 83 percent of the city's small firms reported being victimized by crime in the preceding three years and that one in five was considering leaving the city as a result, while 11 percent said that they had scrapped expansion plans.

By 2000 the story was dramatically different, as the revival of a two-mile strip of Franklin Avenue in Crown Heights shows. Drug dealers had taken over much of the Brooklyn strip by the early 1990s, driving away stores and frightening residents. But by the end of 1996, crime had fallen 45 percent, and hopeful local residents and community groups began to visit owners of boarded-up storefronts and encourage them to try to lease their properties again. Slowly, stores began coming back to life. "In our first sixteen months we attracted twenty-two new stores," says Evangeline Porter, head of the community association in the mostly black neighborhood. Many of these stores belonged to local residents who liked what they saw happening around them. Ann Marie Fraser, an accountant who had lived in the neighborhood for twenty years but operated a storefront tax service elsewhere in Brooklyn, decided to relocate to Franklin Avenue in 1999. "I could see the changes in the neighborhood, like the new residents—white, Asian, Latino. We hadn't seen anything like that in years," she says now. Fraser's was the first new business on a block with four boarded-up stores. Now all the other shops have been rented, too. "I'm hoping for five hundred new clients this tax season," Fraser says.

New York accomplished all this even while it was abandoning a Dinkins-era program to aid minorities through affirmative-action contracting, which gave minority firms an advantage in securing city work. Mayor Giuliani ended the city's minority contracting program in 1994, claiming that such special perquisites were unfair and ineffective in helping minority firms. Instead, he argued, minority firms would benefit from a better overall economic climate, and he was undeniably correct. In the mid-1990s, minority businesses in New York spectacularly outperformed those in cities with minority contracting quotas and preferences. In Houston, for instance, a city that has emphasized set-aside programs for seventeen years, the ranks of minority entrepreneurs increased a wan 11 percent between 1993 and 1997, compared with the 80 percent gain in New York. In Atlanta, two decades of set-aside programs have bene-fited only the small group of privileged vendors who land plum government contracts. Atlanta's minority businesses and sole proprietors increased at only half the pace of New York's gain in the last economic census.

Despite these enormous success stories, the city's busi-ness community has faced a reversal of fortune. Giuliani's successor, Mayor Michael Bloomberg, quickly abandoned a no-tax-hikes pledge made during his campaign and to-gether with a radicalized city council enacted billions of dollars in new taxes. The council also quickly ratified into law a raft of anti-business measures, including new living-wage legislation. The city's economy lost 200,000 jobs in the two years after 9/11 and is again underperforming the na-tional economy. More than 2,000 businesses, most of them small ones, have disappeared in that time. New York City, in short, is going back to the old days of steadily rising taxes and increasing regulation. The city's business community, including its vigorously expanding minority community, is the worse for it already.

It is unclear whether policymakers even notice the auspicious blossoming of the local minority business community that has occurred, much less understand what fostered it—and how crucial it is to the city in so many ways. To keep nurturing these entrepreneurs, lawmakers must first of all do no harm to them. Then they should hack away at taxes and regulations to make New York an easier, more profitable place to do business. Never have minority entrepreneurs—and the city they enrich—had so much to gain, or to lose, from what city and state leaders do next.

Index

Activist policing: crime, reduction of, 19
African-American Teachers Association, 120
Albany (New York), 100
Alcohol and drug addiction programs, 14, 19
Alinsky, Saul, 24
Allen, Jay, 67
American Express, 137
American Federation of State, County, and Municipal Employees (AFSCME), 10; membership, rise in, 11
American Federation of Teachers: and collective bargaining rights, 11; membership, rise in, 11
Ancel, Judy, 39
AOL Time Warner, 137
Archer, Dennis, 27
Ark Restaurants, 136
Arrington, Ted, 116
Association for Community Reform Now (ACORN), 18, 23, 24, 26, 27, 34, 35, 40, 51, 52, 120, 123; hypocrisy of, 33

Atlanta (Georgia), 146
Austin (Texas), 94, 95, 97, 99, 102; artists, support of, 98
Avella, Anthony, 127, 128

Ball State University, 82
Baltimore (Maryland), 22, 58; economic collapse of, 23; strikes in, 11
Barnes, Kay, 17
Barron, Charles, 118, 122, 129, 130, 131; and slavery reparations, 123
Baudelaire, Charles, 93
Bearak, Corey, 128
Beck, Sharie, 61
Bennett, James, 49
Bentonville (Arkansas), 53
Berkeley (California), 45
Berman, Herb, 121
Beverly Hills (California), 25
Bloomberg, Michael, 17, 35, 112, 121, 127, 128, 146; administration of, 125; and Hispanics, 116; and nonpartisan elections, 107, 115

Bobos in Paradise (Brooks), 95
Bohemian Index, 92. *See also*
  Richard Florida; *The Rise of
  the Creative Class.*
Boston (Massachusetts), 26, 27
Bowie, Jim, 98
Brewer, Gale, 120
Broadway Deli (Santa Monica),
  45–46
Brooks, David, 95–96
Buffett, Warren, 57
Bureau of Labor Statistics, 13
Bush, George W., 121, 131
Business owners, 17; and
  workers, 27
Business Week: on Wal-Mart, 65,
  66

California, 20, 33, 36, 40, 63;
  supermarket industry of, 59,
  60, 64
Campbell, Jane, 17
Canada, 98, 106
Cannondale Associates, 66
Carnegie Mellon University, 92
Carter, Jimmy, 13
Carver Bank, 138
Catholic Charities, 12
Cato Institute, 104
Center on Policy Initiatives, 60
Chase Manhattan, 34
Chen, Thomas, 133, 142, 143
Chest, Mose, 142
Chicago (Illinois), 13
Chin, Randy, 141
Chin, Vincent and Patricia, 141
Cincinnati (Ohio), 18, 97
Cincinnati Tomorrow, 97
Cities: creative workers in, 90,
  91; and urban health, 134
Citizens Action, 23
City Journal, 17, 129
City University of New York, 123

Clark, Bob, 55
Clergy and Laity United for
  Economic Justice (CLUE), 25
Clinton, Bill, 75, 122
Clinton, Hillary, 120
Cloward, Richard A., 72, 73, 74
Cohen, Milstein, Hausfeld, and
  Toll, 68
Collective bargaining rights: of
  municipal workers, 10
Communications Workers of
  America, 41
Community-based
  organizations, 18
Community Reinvestment Act, 34
Comrie, Leroi, 128
Corporations: as evil, 43
Creative class, 90, 94, 102; as
  capitalist class, 96; circular
  logic, as basis of, 101; cities
  of, 92, 94, 99, 100, 101, 102,
  103; and cultural amenities,
  91, 103; cultural institutions,
  public funding of, 96; and
  diversity, 95; economics of,
  91, 105, 106; and fast-
  growing businesses, 101;
  inconsistencies of, 102; and
  job growth, 99, 100, 101; and
  lifestyle amenities, 92, 95;
  and population loss, 103; and
  social legislation, 91, 95; and
  urban policymaking, 93, 94,
  95; work, attitude toward, 96
Creative Class Index, 92
Creativity Index, 99, 103
Criminal laws: liberalization of,
  19
Cross-Lines Cooperative, 17
Crystal Door and Window, 142,
  143
C&S Leather Products, 142
Culture wars, 49

Dallas (Texas), 115
Day-care centers, 12
Dayton (Ohio), 100
De Blasio, Bill, 120
Democratic party, 108, 109, 113, 116; and public-sector candidates, 112; and Working Families Party (WFP), 115
DeSapio, Carmine, 108, 109
Detroit (Michigan), 24, 26, 27, 36, 46, 47, 102
Detroit Regional Chamber of Commerce, 26, 27
Díaz, Rubén, 113
Dickman, Howard, 44
Dinkins, David, 118, 145; administration of, 143; and small businesses, 143
Discount industry: and unions, 58. *See also* Wal-Mart.
Duluth (Minnesota), 18
Dylan, Bob, 93

Edison Schools, 34
Education, 86
Ehrenreich, Barbara, 71, 73, 74, 75, 76, 78, 83, 86; as condescending, 81; and middle class, 81; at Wal-Mart, 79, 80
E. J. Korvette chain, 53
Eliot, T. S., 93
Elman, Richard, 72
Empire Foundation, 103
Employee-training programs, 12
Employment Policies Institute, 48
Espada, Pedro, Jr., 111, 112, 113, 114
Ethnic profiling, 130
Europe, 97
Evergreen State College, 49

Fast Company magazine, 95
Fear of Falling: The Inner Life of the Middle Class (Ehrenreich), 74, 80
Florida Education Reform Initiative, 66
Florida International University, 48
Florida, Richard, 90, 91, 92, 93, 94, 95, 102, 103; theories of, 96, 97, 98, 99, 100, 101, 104, 105, 106. *See also* Creative class; *The Rise of the Creative Class.*
Fongemie, Jackie, 52
Food stores: and grocery departments, 58
Ford Foundation, 25
Fortune magazine, 66
Franklin, Cynthia, 137
Fraser, Ann Marie, 145
Freeman, Harry, 63
Free-market economy, 135; and living-wage movement, 28
Free trade, 46
Fresh Democracy Council, 122, 128

Gallagher, Dennis, 129
Gates, Gary, 92
Gay communities: and technology centers, 92
Gender studies, 49–50
General Electric, 87
Gingrich, Newt, 16
Gioia, Eric, 120
Giuliani, Rudy, 9, 17, 23, 34, 116, 117, 130, 134, 144, 146
Giuliani administration, 104, 105, 144; undermining of, 129, 130
Globalization, 44, 46, 87
Gore, Al, 120

Gotbaum, Victor, 109
Grand Rapids (Michigan), 102
Grant, Lloyd, 133, 137
Grisham, John, 81
Grocery sales: and Wal-Mart, 59
Grocery unions: and health-
insurance premiums, 64
Growing Up Fast (Lipper), 87

Harrington, Michael, 70, 71, 72
Hartford (Connecticut), 51
Hartford, Connecticut,
Economic Development
Council, 63
Harvard University, 45
Health-care system, 14;
government takeover of, 15
Health-care unions, 16
Health clinics, 12
Heartland Labor Forum (radio
program), 49
Hoffa, Jimmy, 55
Homeless: programs for, 13
Hospitals, 15; as power bloc, 16
Housing and Urban
Development, 36
Housing groups, 12
Houston, Sam, 98
Houston (Texas), 99; and set-
aside programs, 146
Hunter, Jeffrey, 26

Industrial Democracy in America
(Dickman), 44
Inner City Oceans, 141
Institute of Industrial Relations,
47
Institute for Justice, 65
Institute for Labor Studies
(University of Missouri–
Kansas City), 39
Iowa, 97, 98
Iraq: war in, 25, 49, 131
Ireland, Patricia, 75

Jackson, Jesse, 34
Jackson, Robert, 120, 131
Johnson, Lyndon, 110;
administration of, 14
Journal of Labor Research, 49
J. P. Morgan, 34

Kelley, Jean, 55
Kern, Jed, 24, 26
Kerry, John, 17, 64
Kip Business Report, The, 137
Kohl's, 58
Krugman, Paul, 29

Labor movement, 50; legislative
agenda of, 46; and
privatization, 42; universities,
co-opting of, 38, 41, 43
Labor studies programs, 38, 39,
41; activism, encouragement
of, 40, 44, 45; corporations, as
evil, 43; as interdisciplinary,
44; internship programs of,
45; and labor movement, 43,
50; partisan nature of, 42; as
propaganda, 49; and service
learning, 44, 45
La Guardia, Fiorello, 108
Las Vegas (Nevada), 99, 100,
102, 103
Left: and sustainable wage, 60.
See also New New Left.
Lehman, Herbert, 108
Limbaugh, Rush, 81
Lindsay, John, 73, 110
Lipper, Joanna, 87, 88
*Living Wage: Building a Fair
Economy, The* (Pollin and
Luce), 27, 28, 29
Living-wage legislation, 10, 19,
20, 24, 31, 32, 33, 46, 48;
expansion of, 35
Living-wage movement, 19, 26,
40; agenda of, 22; beginnings

of, 22, 23; and coalition building, 24, 25; economic health, as threat to, 21; free-market economy, rejection of, 28; and labor groups, 25; and morality, 29; at national level, 30; and private sector, 28; religion, use of, 25; and sustainable economics, 36, 37; tactics of, 26, 27

Los Angeles (California), 17, 31, 32, 58, 61, 62

Los Angeles County Economic Development Corporation, 61

Los Angeles Urban League, 62

Lowi, Theodore, 110

Luce, Stephanie, 27, 28, 29, 30

McKnight, Michael, 82

McQueen, Sheila, 138, 139

Mah, Nancy, 136, 137

Maloney, Carolyn, 122

Manhattan Institute, 17, 66

Mansfield University, 82

Mapping America's Entrepreneurial Landscape, 101

Mean Season: The Attack on the Welfare State, The (Cloward, Piven, and Ehrenreich), 73

Medgar Evers College, 123

Medicaid, 14, 15, 16, 63

Medicare, 14, 15, 16

Megatoys Inc., 57

Me Generation, 74

Memphis (Tennessee), 90, 99, 100, 103

Merrill Lynch, 137

Messinger, Ruth, 120

Michael Jordan's Steakhouse, 136

Microsoft, 57

Middle classes, 74

Millard, Charles, 122

Miller, George, 60, 63

Miller, Gifford, 121, 122, 123, 128, 131

Milton and Rose D. Friedman Foundation, 66

Milwaukee (Wisconsin), 36

Minimum wage, 23; and cost of living, 60; and First Amendment, 33. *See also* Living-wage legislation; Living-wage movement.

Minneapolis (Minnesota), 94–95

Money magazine, 105

Moody, Scott, 106

Moore, Stephen, 104

Moynihan, Daniel Patrick, 109

Mugabe, Robert, 123

Municipal unions: and living-wage legislation, 33

Murray, Glen, 98, 106

Nader, Ralph, 23, 75

National Center for Neighborhood Enterprise, 35

National Commission on Entrepreneurship, 101, 102

National Organization for Women, 52, 75

National Right to Work Legal Defense and Education Foundation, 65

Newark (New Jersey): strikes in, 11

New economy, 91, 92; and creative class, 93, 94, 97, 102, 104

New New Left, 18, 20, 134; coalition of, 16; hypocrisy of, 33

New Orleans (Louisiana), 24, 99

Newton (Arkansas), 53

Newton, Isaac, 93

New York City, 9, 11, 13, 15, 23, 94, 97, 102, 104, 105; and affirmative action contracting, 145–146; Board of Estimate, dismantling of, 119; business community of, 123, 127, 128, 129, 139, 140, 146, 147; budget crisis in, 118; city council of, 118, 119, 123, 124, 125, 126, 127, 128, 129, 130, 131, 132; and displaced-worker bill, 124, 125, 128; election-law change in, 112; and health-care workers, 35, 36; immigration to, 140; job losses in, 129, 146; living-wage legislation in, 115, 124, 128, 146; minority businesses in, 133, 134, 135, 136, 137, 139, 140, 142, 144, 146, 147; neighborhood revival in, 142; police department, and racial profiling, 130; politics in, 107, 108, 111, 114, 116, 119; population loss of, 103; and predatory lenders, 125, 126; public-sector domination of, 117, 119, 120; and rent control, 126, 127; small businesses, collapse of in, 143, 144; small-business revival in, 138; social-services organizations, growth of, 110–111; and taxes, 127, 146; and teacher's union, 34; and term limits, 112, 120, 132; welfare-to-work program, weakening of, 130
New York State, 13, 16
New York State Public Employees Federation, 120
New York Times, 117
New Zealand, 97

Nickel and Dimed (Ehrenreich), 71, 75, 76, 79, 83; and middle class, 80, 81; success of, 81, 82
Nonprofit sectors, 18
North America, 97

Oakland (California), 35, 45
Ocean Hill-Brownsville crisis, 120
Ohio State, 82
Oklahoma City (Oklahoma), 99, 100
Organized labor, 20, 50
Other America, The (Harrington), 70
Out-migration, 103; and tax rates, 104

Palma, Annabel, 113, 114
Pariser, Neil, 139
Parks, Bernard, 62
Pataki, George, 123
Patronage, 110; and neighborhood political clubs, 108, 109
Perkins, Bill, 124, 130, 131
Philadelphia (Pennsylvania), 13, 58
Pipette Technologies, 139
Pittsburgh (Pennsylvania), 90, 92, 95
Pittsfield (Massachusetts), 87, 88
Piven, Frances Fox, 72, 73, 74
Playboy magazine: on Wal-Mart, 66
Pollin, Robert, 27, 28, 29, 32; national living wage, proposal of, 30
Poor: civil rights of, 72; and victimization, 72; as victims, 71, 72. *See also* Poverty; Working poor.
Porter, Evangeline, 145

Poverty, 46, 75; and bad choices, 83, 84, 88; and dysfunctional behavior, 83, 88; and government programs, 70, 71, 72; and immigrants, 29; and Me Generation, 74. *See also* Poor; War on Poverty.
Poverty rates, 79; and mobility, 78
Preamble Center for Public Policy, 22
Private sector, 9; workers of, 17
Providence (Rhode Island), 25, 90
Privatization, and labor, 42, 43
Public-employee unions, 12, 16, 109; organization of, 11; and right to strike, 10
Public policy: and urban America, 16
Public-sector movement, 112; in cities, as New Left, 116; as coalition, 111; expansion of, 9; power of, 10; right, to organize, 39; voters of, 18. *See also* Social-service groups.
Public unions, 39; rise of, 110. *See also* Unions.

Queens Civic Congress, 128
Queens College of the City University of New York, 44, 49

Race studies, 50
Racial profiling, 130
Ramos, Nic, 45
Reagan administration, 13; welfare spending, cuts of, 72
Reagan, Ronald, 122
Reed, Philip, 118
Rent Stabilization Association, 125
Reynolds, David, 24, 26, 47
Richmond (Virginia), 106

Rios, Aaron, 61
Rise of the Creative Class, The (Florida), 91, 93, 95
Rivera, Dennis, 16
Rivera, Joe, 139
Rockwell Group, 136
Rogers (Arkansas), 53
Roosevelt, Eleanor, 108
Ruby Foo's, 136

Sacramento (California), 37
Salvation Army, 24, 46, 47
Sander, Richard, 31, 32
San Diego (California), 60, 99, 102
San Francisco (California), 24, 35, 45, 47, 94, 99, 103, 104
San Francisco City Council, 47
San Francisco State University, 47
Santa Monica (California), 25, 32, 33, 45, 46
Schmoke, Kurt, 22
Schweikart, Larry, 82
Scrub Clean, 138
Securities Industry Association, 121
Service Employees International Union, 12
Shanker, Albert, 109
Sharpton, Al, 34
Shipler, David, 71, 83, 84, 85, 86, 87, 88
Silicon Valley, 95
Small Business Congress, 144
Smith, Charles, 137
Social-service groups, 16; and federal spending, 12, 14; growth of, 12, 110–111; and health-care workers' union, 113; as political force, 14, 110; public funding of, 12, 13; and War on Poverty, 12. *See also* Public-sector movement.

South Bronx Overall Economic Development Corporation, 139

Southeastern Michigan Salvation Army, 27

Sphere Institute, 29, 77

Stern, Henry, 119

Stewart, Martha, 81

St. Petersburg (Florida), 18

Strasburg, Joseph, 125

Strikes, 11

Stokes, Arch, 33

Supermarket chains: and unions, 58, 59

Sustainable wage: and the left, 60

Sweeney, John, 38, 41, 43

Tammany Hall, 18, 107

Tampa Bay (Florida), 103

Target, 58

Tax eaters, 17, 20; and political campaigns, 18

Tax Foundation, 106

Teamsters, 55

Technology explosion: and creative class, 93

Teen pregnancy: shame, demise of, 88

Texaco, 68

Tides Foundation, 25

Time magazine, 74

Tweed, Boss, 108

Union of Radical Political Economists, 27

Unions, 10, 18, 39; academics, bond between, 42; decline in, 28; and discount industry, 58; and strikes, 109; and supermarket chains, 58, 60, 64; and Wal-Mart, 59, 62

United Association for Labor Education, 41

United Federation of Teachers, 112

United Food and Commercial Workers Union, 51

Universities: and labor movement, 38, 41; union causes, support of, 46

University of California at Berkeley, 42, 47

University of California's Institute for Labor and Employment, 48

University of California at Los Angeles, 45

University of California at Riverside, 82

University of Illinois at Urbana, 42

University of Massachusetts at Amherst, 40, 42, 43, 45

University of Massachusetts at Boston, 44, 49

University of Massachusetts at Lowell, 49

University of Michigan's Panel Study of Income Dynamics, 78

University of Missouri–Kansas City, 49

University of North Carolina at Chapel Hill, 82

University professors: union movement, as advocates for, 42

Urban America: as leftish, 16

Urban Institute, 77, 78

Urban left, 18, 19

Urban underclass, 73

Vallone, Peter, 119, 122

Vann, Al, 118, 120

Vaughan, Stevie Ray, 98

Velez, Ramon, 14, 111

Villaraigosa, Antonio, 16–17
VP Music, 141

Wagner, Robert, 10, 11
Walker, Anita, 96
Wal-Mart, 9–10, 20, 69, 79, 80,
    81; admiration for, 66;
    benefits of, 61; boycotting of,
    59; corporate culture of, 54,
    55; and grocery sales, 59;
    growth of, 53; health
    insurance plan of, 63; and
    illegal aliens, 67; influence of,
    57; innovations of, 56, 57;
    inventory system of, 56, 57;
    lawsuits against, 67, 68; and
    minority communities, 62;
    opposition to, 52, 53; press
    attacks on, 51, 64, 65, 66;
    profit-sharing program of, 55;
    as revolutionary, 54, 56, 58;
    super centers of, 58;
    supermarket industry, effect
    on, 60; support of, 62; and
    sustainable wages, 60, 61;
    unions, as threat to, 59, 62;
    urban prototype of, 58, 62;
    and women, 68
Wal-Mart Litigation Project, 67
Walton, John, 65
Walton, Sam, 54, 55, 56, 64, 65,
    68–69; beginning of, 53;
    values of, 66
War on Poverty, 12, 14, 18, 19, 70,
    72, 110; failure of, 71, 73, 89

Warner, Philson, 133, 140, 141
Washington, D.C.: public school
    system of, 86
Wayne State University, 40, 42,
    46, 48; living-wage movement,
    as aligned with, 47
Welfare, 19; as continuous, 72;
    reform of, 73, 74, 75, 78, 79,
    89
Weprin, David, 121, 124, 128
Weprin, Saul, 121
Williamstown (Massachusetts),
    87
Winnipeg (Manitoba), 98, 106
Wolfe, Tom, 74
Women's Resource Center, 17
WomenSpace, 17
Woo, Charlie, 57
Woodson, Robert L., 34
Working Families Party (WFP),
    120, 121, 123; power of, 114,
    115
Working poor, 76; and earned-
    income tax credits, 31;
    mobility of, 77, 78. *See also*
    Poor; Poverty; Poverty rates.
Working Poor, The (Shipler), 71,
    83
WSL Strategic Retail, 66, 69

Youngstown (Ohio): strikes in,
    11

Zeidler, Marvin, 45

A NOTE ON THE AUTHOR

Steven Malanga is a senior fellow at The Manhattan Institute in New York City and a contributing editor of *City Journal*, where he writes about the intersection of urban economies, business communities, and public policy. Born in Newark, New Jersey, he grew up there and studied at St. Vincent's College and at the University of Maryland. For fourteen years he was with *Crain's New York Business*, the last seven as executive editor and as a weekly columnist. He has also written for the *Wall Street Journal*, the *New York Times*, the *New York Daily News*, the *New York Post*, and other publications.